MAISON KAYSER'S
FRENCH PASTRY WORKSHOP

ERIC KAYSER

PHOTOGRAPHS BY MASSIMO PESSINA
WITH BLANDINE BOYER

BLACK DOG
& LEVENTHAL
PUBLISHERS
NEW YORK

Copyright © 2017 by Larousse

Translated by Zachary R. Townsend

Cover design by Amanda Kain

Cover copyright © 2017 by Hachette Book Group, Inc.

Hachette Book Group supports the right to free expression and the value of copyright. The purpose of copyright is to encourage writers and artists to produce the creative works that enrich our culture.

The scanning, uploading, and distribution of this book without permission is a theft of the author's intellectual property. If you would like permission to use material from the book (other than for review purposes), please contact permissions@hbgusa.com. Thank you for your support of the author's rights.

Black Dog & Leventhal Publishers
Hachette Book Group
1290 Avenue of the Americas
New York, NY 10104

www.hachettebookgroup.com
www.blackdogandleventhal.com

Originally published in 2014 by Larousse in France under the title *L'Atelier Gourmand d'Éric Kayser*

First Edition: September 2017

Black Dog & Leventhal Publishers is an imprint of Hachette Books, a division of Hachette Book Group. The Black Dog & Leventhal Publishers name and logo are trademarks of Hachette Book Group, Inc.

The publisher is not responsible for websites (or their content) that are not owned by the publisher.

The Hachette Speakers Bureau provides a wide range of authors for speaking events. To find out more, go to www.HachetteSpeakersBureau.com or call (866) 376-6591.

Print book interior design by Émilie Franc

Library of Congress Cataloging-in-Publication Data has been applied for.

ISBNs: 978-0-316-43927-5 (hardcover), 978-0-316-47364-4 (ebook)

Printed in China

1010

10 9 8 7 6 5 4 3 2 1

Contents

Les Tartes

La Fameuse Pâte à Choux

Les Incontournables

Les Macarons

Les Gâteaux de Fêtes

Les Gâteaux sans Gluten

Foreword

In 1996, I opened my first boulangerie in Paris on rue Monge. Little did I know then that it would be one of the premier places in the world for great bread. It had been my desire to share these yeast-leavened breads—with their fragrance of toasted grains, and whose flavors I associate with my childhood—with everyone. And since that first boulangerie, I have never stopped imparting my expertise for bread-making, from Paris to Tokyo, New York to Singapore, with the goal of making excellent, beautiful, and real bread accessible to all those who have an appreciation for great food.

This desire to share and teach is the raison d'être of Les Compagnons du Devoir, a centuries-old artisans' guild in France to which I belong, dedicated to the sharing of one's craft through training. These principles have always stayed with me, from the boulangerie school where I was an instructor to the core values of the Maison Kayser bakeries. "Learn and teach" could be my motto, because I view every day as an opportunity to be either pupil or teacher.

This book is a representation of this philosophy. What I have learned I hope to pass on to the greatest number of people. Through these recipes—both simple and complex—I offer passionate bakers the means to satisfy their gourmet cravings. Whether as a treat to enjoy alone or to share with others, there is something here for all tastes! Loaves, tarts, financiers, cookies, macarons, and madeleines are easy-to-make items to take with you to the office or on a picnic, while elaborate desserts such as Fraisier, Opéra, Charlotte, Mille-Feuille, and Saint-Honoré are elegant finishes to meals with friends and family.

My wish is that this book will serve as a simple tool that will, step by step, guide those who want to create from their own hands something sweet for sharing and out of friendship. And, so that everyone can enjoy these pleasures, I have included a chapter of gluten-free recipes.

So, for all bakers—young or old, expert or amateur—let's begin...happiness awaits at the tip of your spatula!

Essential Tips
FOR BAKING SUCCESS

Our recipes were adapted so that they could easily be made at home. They range from the simplest cookies and loaves ideal for snacking and making with children to the most elaborate cakes perfect for celebrations or holidays with family. And, if while thumbing through this book you have a sudden craving for madeleines or chouquettes, here are several important points to keep in mind before donning your apron.

EQUIPMENT
Cake Molds and Pans
This is an important point that bears repeating: High-quality cake molds and pans are worth the investment!
• Choose those made of stainless steel and always dry them thoroughly between uses (you can briefly place them in an already-warm oven) and routinely and generously grease them.
• Nonstick pans are tempting to use, but you must be willing to treat them with tender care—be careful that someone does not slice the tart while it's still in the pan or else risk scratches.
• As for silicone molds, these are a matter of personal preference, but are not necessarily practical for large baked goods, especially when you forget to place them on a baking sheet before filling them. What's more, unmolding a tart from a large silicone mold can be a tricky process. On the other hand, silicone molds are indispensable, even unmatched, for single-serving recipes such as financiers (see pages 36 to 42) and other small, fragile cakes. To perfectly unmold the Mi-cuit au Chocolat found on pages 36 to 42, carefully push up from the bottom of the mold using two fingers so that they pop out with ease. A silicone sheet pan with a depth of about ⅓ inch (1 cm) is equally useful. To test the quality of silicone, discreetly scratch it with your fingernail; it should not leave a mark.
• Do not use glass or ceramic pans when a crisp, browned crust is essential. Instead, keep these for other baked desserts, such as clafoutis.

Baking Sheets
When lined with parchment paper, a rimmed sheet pan (half-sheet, 13 x 18 inches, [33 x 46 cm] can be used for baking the sponge cakes in this book. For cookies and other items usually produced in batches, two rimless baking sheets are useful when you want to bake on two different oven racks at the same time.

Electric Mixers
If you make desserts and pastries often, a heavy-duty standing mixer is indispensable, preferably one with both paddle (flat) and whisk attachments. If you do not have a standing mixer, then a handheld mixer and a little extra time and arm endurance when mixing the ingredients will achieve the same result.

Immersion Blenders
This is a valuable tool for puréeing, as its ability to produce a silky texture by perfectly emulsifying mixtures, such as creams containing gelatin or butter, is unrivaled.

Cake Rings
Without these essential tools (which until recently were only used by, and available to, professionals) constructing multi-layered cakes with delicate fillings would be nearly impossible, as they make unmolding easy. One adjustable round and/or square cake ring will bring a professional look to your Fraisier or Succès, making them ready for competition!

MISCELLANEOUS SMALL EQUIPMENT
The following tools are also essential for anyone serious about baking:
• One or two silicone spatulas, one very soft and one semi-soft.
• One or two whisks, ideally one large and one small.
• At least two pastry brushes (made of silicone, or paintbrushes made of fine, natural bristles).
• One of the brushes should be reserved for fatty mixtures. The brushes should be dishwasher safe.

• One small metal spatula, flat or offset, for spreading fillings.

• Two or three washable plastic pastry bags (fabric bags tend to dry poorly and absorb odors). Alternatively, use disposable pastry bags.

• A variety of pastry tubes (also called pastry tips; at least three plain tubes of different diameters and two sizes of open star tubes), either stainless steel or plastic. Helpful sizes for the recipes in this book include 1/3-in (#3), 1/2-in (#6), 5/8-in (#8), 11/16-in (#9) round; 5/8-in (#8) French star; and 9/16-in (#7) open star.

Specialized Equipment

• For éclairs and cream puffs: plain long pastry tubes (small and large bismark tubes) for piping fillings into the pastries.

• For Saint-Honoré and yule logs: Saint-Honoré tube (9/16-in notched tube) and yule log pastry tube (7/8-in flat, serrated tube).

• An instant-read thermometer: for testing cakes for doneness.

• A candy thermometer: for testing caramel and syrups (instructions are also provided in the recipes for the traditional cold-water method of estimating the temperature of a hot syrup).

• An oven thermometer: if your oven's thermostat is not reliable (temperatures and cooking times indicated in the recipes should be adjusted according to your oven's temperature variations).

• Ceramic pie weights: for prebaking pastry crusts.

• Metal yule log pans: can be found in professional pastry shops, or purchase less expensive plastic ones online under the description "plastic yule log mold."

METHODS

Prebaking (or Blind Baking)

This is an effective approach for avoiding soggy tart crusts and preventing dough from shrinking during baking. Follow the step-by-step instructions on page 62 for this method. Ceramic pie weights are preferred over dried beans, which become too light after several uses. You can also use small pebbles that have been thoroughly washed. Refrigerating the dough after transferring it to the pan is also very helpful in ensuring it keeps its shape.

Patience

Read through all of the recipe directions first. It is not a good idea to attempt to complete, in one day, a multi-layered cake or one that contains a center layer that must firm up. Begin as many steps as possible the day before serving and pay close attention to the timing indicated for each step—this is critical for ensuring creams have set properly before use. Once assembled, most of these cakes must rest in the refrigerator or freezer for several hours—or ideally overnight—until fully set. (Recipes that use puff or choux pastry are the exception; these soften with continued refrigeration).

Saving Time

The quantities in many of the recipes in this book can be doubled or tripled, then frozen until needed, such as crumbly sweet pastry dough (pâte sablée) or puff pastry dough, which both freeze very well. Simply divide the dough before storing it or, better still, roll it out onto parchment paper, then roll it up in the paper to store it (as is done with store-bought doughs).

If you have many tart pans, you can line them with the dough then freeze them, stacked and tightly wrapped, ready to fill and bake when needed.

For cookies, keep the cookie dough logs in the freezer, then set them out to thaw slightly before slicing off the desired number of pieces to be baked.

Les Gâteaux de Tous les Jours

EVERYDAY LOAVES AND CAKES

Cake à la Pistache et aux Griottes

PISTACHIO AND CHERRY LOAF CAKE

★ ★ ★

SERVES
6 to 8

PREPARATION TIME: 15 minutes · COOKING TIME: 45 minutes
One loaf pan measuring 8 ½ in (22 cm) by 4 ½ in (11.5 cm)

FOR THE BATTER: 1 cup plus 2 tsp (7 ½ oz/210 g) granulated sugar · 3 large (5 ¼ oz/150 g) eggs · 2 tbsp plus 2 tsp (1 ½ oz/40 g) unsalted butter · 2 cups minus 2 tbsp (6 ½ oz/185 g) all-purpose flour · ¾ tsp plus ⅛ tsp (¹⁄₁₀ oz/3 g) baking powder · 2 pinches salt · ¼ cup plus 2 ½ tbsp (100 mL) heavy whipping cream · 2 ½ oz (70 g) pistachio paste · 2 ½ oz (70 g) frozen Morello cherries
FOR THE SYRUP: 1 tbsp (½ oz/13 g) granulated sugar · 1 tsp (5 mL) kirsch (cherry liqueur)

* Preheat the oven to 325°F/165°C. Grease and flour the loaf pan.
* Place the sugar and eggs in a large mixing bowl or in the bowl of a standing mixer fitted with the whisk attachment and beat for several minutes on medium-low speed, just until foamy.
* Melt the butter.
* Sift together the flour, baking powder, and salt. Add the flour mixture to the beaten eggs and mix gently, just until combined. Add the cream, melted butter, and pistachio paste, beating just until combined after each addition. Fold in the frozen cherries using a silicone spatula.

* Scrape the batter into the prepared pan and bake for 30 minutes. Lower the oven temperature to 300°F/145°C and bake for another 15 minutes, or until golden (210°F/100°C on an instant-read thermometer). Do not overbake.
* Meanwhile, make the syrup. In a small saucepan, bring the sugar, kirsch, and 2 tbsp (30 mL) water to a boil, then remove from the heat and let cool. As soon as the cake comes out of the oven, brush it with the syrup using a pastry brush.
* Place the cake on a wire rack to cool for several minutes before unmolding.

Cake au Citron Confit

CANDIED LEMON LOAF CAKE

★★★

SERVES
6 to 8

PREPARATION TIME: 15 minutes · COOKING TIME: 45 minutes
One loaf pan measuring 8 ½ in (22 cm) by 4 ½ in (11.5 cm)

FOR THE LEMON PASTE: 1 ¼ oz (35 g) candied lemon peel · 1 tbsp (15 mL) freshly squeezed lemon juice (from ½ lemon) · 1 ½ tsp (¹⁄₁₀ oz/3 g) freshly grated lemon zest (from ½ lemon)

FOR THE BATTER: 1 cup (7 oz/200 g) granulated sugar · 3 large (5 ¼ oz/150 g) eggs · ¾ stick plus 2 tsp (3 ¹⁄₃ oz/95 g) unsalted butter · 2 cups minus 3 tbsp (6 ¹⁄₃ oz/180 g) all-purpose flour · 1 ¼ tsp (⅛ oz/5 g) baking powder · ¼ cup plus 2 ½ tbsp (100 mL) heavy whipping cream

FOR THE SYRUP: 1 tbsp (½ oz/13 g) granulated sugar · 2 tbsp (30 mL) freshly squeezed lemon juice (from 1 lemon)

FOR THE DECORATION: 1 ½ oz (40 g) candied lemon peel, in strips

* Preheat the oven to 325°F/165°C. Grease and flour the loaf pan.

* Make the lemon paste. In a food processor, combine the lemon peel, lemon juice, and zest and process until almost smooth.

* Make the batter. Place the sugar and eggs in a large mixing bowl or in the bowl of a standing mixer fitted with the whisk attachment and beat for several minutes on medium-low speed, just until foamy.

* Melt the butter.

* Sift together the flour and the baking powder. Add the flour mixture to the beaten eggs and mix gently, just until combined. Add the cream, melted butter, and lemon paste, beating just until combined after each addition.

* Scrape the batter into the prepared pan and bake for 30 minutes. Lower the oven temperature to 300°F/145°C and bake for another 15 minutes, or until golden (210°F/100°C on an instant-read thermometer). Do not overbake.

* Meanwhile, make the syrup. In a small saucepan, bring the sugar, lemon juice, and 2 tbsp (30 mL) water to a boil, then remove from the heat and let cool. As soon as the cake comes out of the oven, brush it with the syrup using a pastry brush.

* Place on a wire rack to cool for several minutes before unmolding. Dice a few strips of the candied lemon peel and place them on top with the whole strips.

Variation: For Cake à l'Orange/Orange Loaf Cake, replace the candied lemon peel, lemon juice, and lemon zest with orange. In the syrup, replace the lemon juice with Grand Marnier orange liqueur.

Cake aux Fruits Confits

CANDIED FRUIT LOAF CAKE

★ ★ ★

SERVES
6 to 8

PREPARATION TIME: 15 minutes · COOKING TIME: 45 minutes
One loaf pan measuring 8 ½ in (22 cm) by 4 ½ in (11.5 cm)

- ⅔ cup plus ½ tsp (4 ¾ oz/135 g) granulated sugar
- 2 large (3 ½ oz/100 g) eggs
- 1 stick minus ¾ tsp (3 ¾ oz/110 g) unsalted butter, room temperature
- 2 ¼ cups minus 1 tbsp (7 ½ oz/215 g) all-purpose flour
- 1 ¼ tsp (⅛ oz/5 g) baking powder
- 2 pinches salt
- ¼ cup (60 mL) whole milk
- 2 tbsp (30 mL) rum
- 9 oz (260 g) mixed candied fruits
- 2 oz (55 g) raisins
- 1 oz (25 g) chopped candied orange peel

＊ Preheat the oven to 325°F/165°C. Grease and flour the loaf pan.

＊ Place the sugar and eggs in a large mixing bowl or in the bowl of a standing mixer fitted with the whisk attachment and beat for several minutes on medium-low speed, just until foamy. Add the butter and beat to combine.

＊ Sift together the flour, baking powder, and salt. Add the flour mixture to the beaten eggs and mix gently, just until combined. Add the milk and rum, beating just until combined after each addition. Fold in the candied fruits, raisins, and orange peel using a silicone spatula.

＊ Scrape the batter into the prepared pan and bake for 30 minutes. Lower the oven temperature to 300°F/145°C and bake for another 15 minutes, or until golden (210°F/100°C on an instant-read thermometer). Do not overbake.

＊ Place the loaf on a wire rack to cool for several minutes before unmolding.

Cake au Pavot et au Citron Vert

LIME AND POPPY SEED LOAF CAKE

★ ★ ★

SERVES
6 to 8

PREPARATION TIME: 15 minutes · COOKING TIME: 45 minutes
One loaf pan measuring 8 ½ in (22 cm) by 4 ½ in (11.5 cm)

- 1 ¼ cups minus 2 tsp (8 ½ oz/240 g) granulated sugar
- 3 large (5 ¼ oz/150 g) eggs
- 2 tbsp plus 2 tsp (1 ½ oz/40 g) unsalted butter, room temperature
- 2 cups minus 2 tbsp (6 ½ oz/185 g) all-purpose flour
- 2 ½ tsp (⅓ oz/10 g) baking powder
- 2 pinches salt
- ¼ cup plus 2 ½ tbsp (100 mL) heavy whipping cream
- 1 tbsp plus 1 tsp (¼ oz/8 g) freshly grated lime zest (from 1 lime)
- 3 tbsp (1 oz/25 g) poppy seeds
- 2 ½ tbsp (40 mL) sunflower oil

* Preheat the oven to 325°F/165°C. Grease and flour the loaf pan.

* Place the sugar and eggs in a large mixing bowl or in the bowl of a standing mixer fitted with the whisk attachment and beat for several minutes on medium-low speed, just until foamy. Add the butter and beat to combine.

* Sift together the flour, baking powder, and salt. Add the flour mixture to the beaten eggs and mix gently, just until combined. Add the cream and mix just until combined. Add the zest, poppy seeds, and oil and mix just until combined.

* Scrape the batter into the prepared pan and bake for 30 minutes. Lower the oven temperature to 300°F/145°C and bake for another 15 minutes, or until golden (210°F/100°C on an instant-read thermometer). Do not overbake.

* Place the loaf on a wire rack to cool for several minutes before unmolding.

Cake Coco-Rhum

COCONUT-RUM LOAF CAKE

SERVES
6 to 8

PREPARATION TIME: 15 minutes · COOKING TIME: 40 minutes
One loaf pan measuring 8 ½ in (22 cm) by 4 ½ in (11.5 cm)

FOR THE BATTER:

- ¾ stick plus 1 tsp (3 ⅛ oz/90 g) unsalted butter, room temperature
- ¾ cup (5 ¼ oz/150 g) granulated sugar
- 2 large (3 ½ oz/100 g) eggs
- 1 ½ cups minus 1 tbsp (5 oz/140 g) all-purpose flour
- ¼ cup plus ¾ tbsp (1 ½ oz/45 g) cornstarch
- 1 ¼ tsp (⅛ oz/5 g) baking powder
- 2 ½ tbsp (40 mL) rum
- 3 tbsp (45 mL) coconut milk
- ¼ cup (60 mL) heavy whipping cream
- 1 cup (2 ½ oz/75 g) grated unsweetened coconut

FOR THE SYRUP:

- 1 tbsp (½ oz/13 g) granulated sugar
- 1 tbsp (15 mL) coconut liqueur, preferably Malibu

FOR THE DECORATION:

- 1 tbsp (⅛ oz/5 g) freshly grated coconut

* Preheat the oven to 350°F/180°C. Grease and flour the loaf pan.

* Place the butter and sugar in a large mixing bowl or in the bowl of a standing mixer fitted with the whisk attachment and beat for several minutes on medium-low speed until very light and creamy. With the mixer running, add the eggs one at a time and beat until combined.

* Sift together the flour, cornstarch, and baking powder. Add the flour mixture to the bowl and mix gently, just until combined. Add the rum, coconut milk, cream, and grated coconut, mixing just until combined after each addition.

* Scrape the batter into the prepared pan and bake for 25 minutes. Lower the oven temperature to 325°F/160°C and bake for another 15 minutes, or until golden (210°F/100°C on an instant-read thermometer). Do not overbake.

* Meanwhile, make the syrup. In a small saucepan, bring the sugar, liqueur, and 2 tbsp (30 mL) water to a boil, then remove from the heat and let cool. As soon as the cake comes out of the oven, brush it with the syrup using a pastry brush.

* Place the loaf on a wire rack to cool for several minutes before unmolding. Sprinkle with grated coconut.

Cake au Chocolat
CHOCOLATE LOAF CAKE

SERVES
6 to 8

PREPARATION TIME: 15 minutes · COOKING TIME: 45 minutes
One loaf pan measuring 8 ½ in (22 cm) by 4 ½ in (11.5 cm)

FOR THE BATTER: 1½ cups plus 1 tbsp plus 2 tsp (5½ oz/160 g) confectioners' sugar, sifted · 1 tbsp plus 1¾ tsp (¾ oz/20 g) granulated sugar · 3 large (5¼ oz/150 g) eggs · 1½ sticks plus 1 tsp (6⅓ oz/180 g) unsalted butter, room temperature · 1⅔ cups (5¾ oz/165 g) all-purpose flour · ½ cup minus 1 tsp (1½ oz/40 g) unsweetened Dutch-process cocoa powder · ¼ cup plus 2 tbsp (1¼ oz/35 g) hazelnut flour · 1¾ tsp plus ⅛ tsp (¼ oz/8 g) baking powder · 2 pinches salt · 1 tbsp (15 mL) heavy whipping cream · 5¾ oz (165 g) dark chocolate, in chips or finely chopped
FOR THE SYRUP: 1 tbsp (½ oz/13 g) granulated sugar · 1 tbsp (15 mL) rum

* Preheat the oven to 325°F/165°C. Grease and flour the loaf pan.
* Place the confectioners' sugar, granulated sugar, and eggs in a large mixing bowl or in the bowl of a standing mixer fitted with the whisk attachment and beat for several minutes on medium-low speed, just until foamy. Add the butter and beat to combine.
* Sift together the flour, cocoa, hazelnut flour, baking powder, and salt. Add the flour mixture to the beaten eggs and mix gently, just until combined. Add the cream and mix just until combined. Fold in the chocolate using a silicone spatula.

* Scrape the batter into the prepared pan and bake for 30 minutes. Lower the oven temperature to 300°F/145°C and bake for another 15 minutes, or until slightly darkened on top (210°F/100°C on an instant-read thermometer). Do not overbake.
* Meanwhile, make the syrup. In a small saucepan, bring the sugar, rum, and 2 tbsp (30 mL) water to a boil, then remove from the heat and let cool. As soon as the cake comes out of the oven, brush it with the syrup using a pastry brush.
* Place the loaf on a wire rack to cool for several minutes before unmolding.

Mi-cuit au Chocolat

MOLTEN CHOCOLATE CAKE

★ ★ ★

SERVES
6 to 8

PREPARATION TIME: 10 minutes · COOKING TIME: 8 to 19 minutes, depending on the size of the cake pan
One 7-in (18-cm) round cake pan or six 3-in (8-cm) round pans or ramekins

1 stick plus 1 tbsp plus 1 tsp (4 ¾ oz/135 g) unsalted butter · 5 ¼ oz (150 g) 65% cacao dark chocolate, in disks or evenly chopped · 4 large (7 oz/200 g) eggs · ¾ cup plus 1 tbsp plus 1¾ tsp (6 oz/170 g) granulated sugar · ½ cup plus 1 tbsp plus 2 tsp (2 ⅛ oz/60 g) all-purpose flour, sifted

❋ Preheat the oven to 375°F/190°C. Grease and flour the cake pan (if using a silicone pan, there is no need to grease or flour it).

❋ Cut the butter into pieces. Place the chocolate and butter in a heatproof bowl set over a pot of simmering water and gently melt them together (or place them in a microwave-safe bowl and microwave for 1 minute), then stir until completely melted. Whisk until smooth then remove from the heat.

❋ In a bowl, whisk together the eggs and sugar until foamy and lightened. Add the egg mixture to the chocolate mixture and whisk until thoroughly combined. Using a silicone spatula, gently incorporate the flour, just until combined.

❋ Scrape the batter into the prepared pan(s) and bake for 15 to 19 minutes for the 7-in (18-cm) pan or 8 to 10 minutes for the 3-in (8-cm) pans.

❋ Cool completely. Carefully unmold onto a wire rack (do not unmold if in ramekins).

Cheesecake

★ ★ ★

SERVES
6 to 8

PREPARATION TIME: 15 minutes · COOKING TIME: 1 hour · REFRIGERATION TIME: Overnight
One springform pan or removable-bottom cake pan, 7 in (18 cm) to 8 in (20 cm) in diameter

FOR THE CRUST: 1 stick minus 2 tsp (3 2/3 oz/105 g) unsalted butter, room temperature · 1/2 cup (3 2/3 oz/105 g) light brown sugar · 1 cup plus 1 tbsp (3 2/3 oz/105 g) all-purpose flour · 3/4 cup (3 2/3 oz/105 g) almond flour
FOR THE FILLING: 6 1/3 oz (180 g) fromage blanc (see Note) · 3/4 cup plus 2 tbsp plus 1 1/4 tsp (6 1/3 oz/180 g) granulated sugar · 14 oz (400 g) Philadelphia brand cream cheese, room temperature · 3 large (5 1/4 oz/150 g) eggs · 1 tsp (5 mL) pure vanilla extract

* Preheat the oven to 300°F/150°C.
* Place the butter and brown sugar in a large bowl (1). Add the all-purpose and almond flours (2). Using your hands, combine the ingredients in the bowl, then turn the mixture out onto a work surface. Continue kneading until the mixture forms a smooth mass (3).
* Place the dough in the pan and, using your fingers, press it evenly along the bottom and carefully up the sides of the pan (4) (5).
* Bake for 10 minutes, or until the edges of the crust are golden (6).
* Meanwhile, in a large mixing bowl, whisk together the fromage blanc, sugar, and cream cheese (7) until very smooth (8). Gradually whisk in the eggs one by one until the mixture is smooth (9). Add the vanilla and whisk to combine (10).
* Lower the oven temperature to 275°F/140°C . Scrape the filling into the pan (11) and bake for about 1 hour, turning off the oven as soon as the filling begins to crack around the edge. (Do not remove the cake from the oven.)
* Let cool completely in the oven, then refrigerate overnight.
* Decorate with seasonal berries (preferably red berries) and serve with a berry coulis.

Note: Full-fat plain Greek yogurt or whole-milk ricotta may be used as a substitute for fromage blanc.

(1)

(2)

(3)

Brownies

PREPARATION TIME: 10 minutes · COOKING TIME: 25 minutes
One 9-in (23-cm) square cake pan or an 8-in (20 cm) by 12-in (30-cm) cake pan,
lined with parchment paper or greased foil (see Note)

- ¾ cup plus 1 tbsp plus 2 ½ tsp (3 oz/85 g) all-purpose flour
- 2 pinches salt
- ¾ tsp plus ⅛ tsp (¹⁄₁₀ oz/3 g) baking powder
- 2 sticks minus 1 tbsp (7 ½ oz/215 g) unsalted butter
- 8 ½ oz (245 g) 60% cacao dark chocolate, in chips or finely chopped
- 4 large (7 oz/200 g) eggs
- 1 ½ cups minus 1 tsp (10 ¼ oz/290 g) granulated sugar
- 1 ⅓ cups (5 ⅛ oz/145 g) walnuts, chopped
- 1 ¼ cups (5 ⅛ oz/145 g) pecan halves

Note: Line the pan with enough parchment paper or greased foil to go all the way up both sides of the pan. The brownies can then be easily lifted out of the pan when warm without breaking them.

* Preheat the oven to 325°F/160°C.

* Sift together the flour, salt, and baking powder.

* In a small saucepan or in a microwave-safe bowl, melt the butter. Remove from the heat and add the chocolate. Set aside for several minutes to allow the chocolate to melt, then whisk until smooth.

* In a large mixing bowl, whisk together the eggs and sugar, then stir in the flour mixture. Stir in the chopped walnuts, then the melted chocolate mixture.

* Scrape the batter into the prepared pan and spread it out evenly. Distribute the pecan halves on top and bake for 25 minutes, or until a toothpick inserted in the center comes out with a few moist crumbs sticking to it. Do not overbake.

* Unmold the brownies from the pan while still warm. Cool completely before slicing.

Pain d'Épices aux Fruits

SPICE CAKE WITH DRIED FRUIT

★ ★ ★

SERVES
6 to 8

PREPARATION TIME: 15 minutes (over 2 days) · COOKING TIME: 1 ½ to 2 hours
One loaf pan measuring 8 in (20 cm) by 4 in (10 cm)

FOR THE SYRUP: ¼ cup plus 2 tbsp plus 1¼ tsp (3 oz/80 g) granulated sugar · Scant
¼ cup (3 oz/80 g) honey · 4 star anise · ¼ tsp (0.5 g) quatre-épices spice blend · ½ cinnamon stick
FOR THE BATTER: 1½ cups minus 1 tbsp (5 oz/140 g) all-purpose flour · 1½ tbsp (½ oz/15 g) potato
starch · 1¼ tsp (⅛ oz/5 g) baking powder · 1 tsp (⅛ oz/5 g) baking soda · 2 tbsp (30 mL) rum · 1 oz
(30 g) dried apricots, diced · 1 oz (30 g) candied orange peel, diced · 1 oz (30 g) pitted prunes,
diced · 3 tbsp (1 oz/30 g) whole almonds, skins removed

* The day before serving, make the syrup. In a saucepan, place all of the syrup ingredients and ½ cup (120 mL) water. Simmer for 5 minutes over low heat. Remove from the heat and set aside, covered, to infuse for 24 hours.

* The next day, strain the syrup through a fine-mesh strainer.

* When ready to bake, preheat the oven to 325°F/160°C. Grease the pan, then line the bottom and sides with parchment paper.

* In a large bowl, whisk together the flour, potato starch, baking powder, and baking soda.

Whisk in the syrup until smooth. Add the rum, dried fruits, and almonds, and stir together using a silicone spatula.

* Scrape the batter into the prepared pan and bake for 1½ to 2 hours (210°F/100°C on an instant-read thermometer). Let the loaf cool slightly, then unmold and let rest for at least 3 to 4 hours before eating, to allow the flavors to develop.

Note: If well wrapped, this cake will keep for up to 10 days.

Gâteau Basque

ALMOND CUSTARD TART

★ ★ ★

SERVES
6 to 8

PREPARATION TIME: 25 minutes · REFRIGERATION TIME: 3 hours · COOKING TIME: 40 minutes
One 9-in (23-cm) round cake pan or eight 4-in (10-cm) round tart pans (see Note)

FOR THE DOUGH: 2 ½ cups (8 ½ oz/245 g) all-purpose flour · 1¾ tsp plus ⅛ tsp (¼ oz/8 g) baking powder · 1 stick plus 3 tbsp (5 ¼ oz/150 g) unsalted butter, room temperature · ¼ cup plus 2 tbsp (2 ½ oz/75 g) granulated sugar · 3 tbsp plus 1 tsp (1 ½ oz/45 g) light brown sugar · 3 tbsp plus 1 tsp (1 oz/30 g) almond flour · 3 large (2 oz/57 g) egg yolks · 2 tsp (10 mL) pure vanilla extract

FOR THE PASTRY CREAM: 1 large (⅔ oz/19 g) egg yolk · 2 tbsp plus 1¼ tsp (1 oz/30 g) granulated sugar · 1 tbsp (⅓ oz/10 g) cornstarch · ⅔ cup (150 mL) whole milk · 1 tbsp plus 1 tsp (¾ oz/20 g) unsalted butter, chilled and cut into pieces

FOR THE ALMOND CREAM: ½ stick plus 1¾ tsp (2 ⅓ oz/65 g) unsalted butter, room temperature · ¼ cup plus 1 tbsp plus ½ tsp (2 ⅓ oz/65 g) granulated sugar · 1 large (1¾ oz/50 g) egg · ½ cup minus 2 tsp (2 ⅓ oz/65 g) almond flour · 1 tbsp (⅓ oz/10 g) cornstarch · ¼ cup (60 mL) rum

FOR FINISHING: 2 large (1⅓ oz/38 g) egg yolks, lightly beaten

✳ **Make the dough.** Sift together the flour and baking powder. Place the remaining ingredients in the bowl of a standing mixer fitted with the paddle attachment and mix for several minutes on low speed until combined. Add the flour mixture and beat on low speed, just until combined. Turn the dough out onto a piece of plastic wrap and form it into a ball. Wrap it with the plastic wrap, then refrigerate for at least 1 hour.

✳ **Make the pastry cream** following the step-by-step instructions on page 138. In a medium bowl, vigorously whisk together the egg yolk and sugar, just until lightened. Whisk in the cornstarch. In a saucepan, warm the milk, then pour it slowly into the egg mixture while whisking constantly. Pour the entire mixture back into the saucepan and cook over medium heat, whisking constantly, until very thick, about 5 minutes. Add the butter pieces to the cream. Using an immersion blender, blend the mixture until smooth and the butter is incorporated. Cover the surface of the cream with plastic wrap and refrigerate for at least 3 hours.

✳ Preheat the oven to 350°F/180°C.

✳ **Make the almond cream.** In the bowl of a standing mixer fitted with the paddle attachment, beat the butter with the sugar until creamy. Add the egg, almond flour, cornstarch, and rum, beating just until combined after each addition. Add the chilled pastry cream to the almond cream and mix to combine.

✳ Divide the dough into two pieces, making one piece twice the size of the other. Roll out the larger piece to about 11 in (28 cm) in diameter and line the pan with it. Scrape the cream mixture into the pan and spread it out evenly.

✳ Roll out the smaller piece into a 9-in (23-cm) circle. Using a pastry brush, brush the edges of the dough circle with the beaten egg yolks, then place it on top of the tart. Press all around the edges of the dough to seal the two layers.

✳ Generously brush the top of the dough with the beaten egg yolk, then let it rest for 10 minutes before baking.

✳ Bake for 40 minutes, or until golden.

Note: For the bottom and top crusts of the 4-in (10-cm) pans, cut out eight 5 ½-in (14-cm) circles for the bottoms and eight 4-in (10-cm) circles for the tops.

Kugelhopf

YEASTED FRUIT BREAD

★ ★ ★

SERVES
12 to 16

PREPARATION TIME: 15 minutes using a standing mixer or 30 minutes using a handheld mixer
PROOFING: 4 to 5 hours · COOKING TIME: 25 to 35 minutes
Two 9-in (23-cm) kugelhopf molds

FOR THE BATTER: 2¾ cups (9⅔ oz/275 g) all-purpose flour · 1 tsp (¼ oz/6 g) salt · ¼ cup plus 1¼ tsp (2 oz/55 g) granulated sugar · 2 tbsp (½ oz/13 g) dry milk powder · ¼ oz (8 g) fresh cake yeast · ⅓ oz (10 g) dried sourdough starter · 2 large (3½ oz/100 g) eggs · 1 stick plus 1 tbsp plus 2 tsp (5 oz/140 g) unsalted butter, room temperature · ½ cup (3 oz/80 g) golden raisins · ¾ cup (3 oz/85 g) slivered almonds
FOR THE DECORATION: 24 whole almonds · ½ cup minus 1 tbsp minus 1 tsp (1½ oz/40 g) confectioners' sugar

* In the bowl of a standing mixer fitted with the paddle attachment, place all of the batter ingredients except the butter, raisins, and almonds.
* Mix on low speed for 5 minutes, then raise the speed to high and beat for another 5 minutes.
* Add the butter and beat for 5 minutes, or until incorporated (if doing this step with a handheld mixer, double the amount of beating time). Mix in the raisins and almonds.
* Cover the dough with a damp towel and place it in a warm spot to rise, 1 hour or until doubled.
* While the dough is rising, generously grease the molds, then place a whole almond in each indentation at the bottom.

* Lightly work the dough to deflate it. Lightly dust a work surface with flour. Cut the dough in half and form it into two balls.
* Using your finger, poke a hole through the middle of each dough ball, then stretch them out to form a ring. Place the dough rings into the molds. Cover and set aside in a warm place. Let rise for 3 to 4 hours or until the dough rises to fill the pans.
* Preheat the oven to 375°F/190°C. Bake for 25 to 35 minutes, or until golden (210°F/100°C on an instant-read thermometer). As soon as the cakes come out of the oven, invert and unmold them onto a wire rack to cool. Dust with confectioners' sugar.

Les Biscuits
TEA CAKES AND COOKIES

Madeleines

BUTTER CAKES

★ ★ ★

**MAKES 30
MADELEINES**

PREPARATION TIME: 10 minutes (over 2 days) · REFRIGERATION TIME: Overnight · COOKING TIME: 17 minutes

Three madeleine pans

- 2 sticks minus 1 tsp (7¾ oz/220 g) unsalted butter
- 2¼ cups (7¾ oz/220 g) all-purpose flour
- 1⅔ tsp (¼ oz/7 g) baking powder
- 1¼ cups (9 oz/250 g) granulated sugar
- 4 large (7 oz/200 g) eggs
- 1 tsp (5 mL) pure vanilla extract

☀ The day before baking, make the batter. Melt the butter. Sift together the flour and baking powder. Place the sugar, eggs, and vanilla in a large mixing bowl or in the bowl of a standing mixer fitted with the whisk attachment and beat until well combined. Add the melted butter and beat until the mixture is smooth.

☀ Ideally, you should grease and flour the molds and fill them, then place them in the refrigerator overnight. You can also place the batter in the refrigerator overnight and fill the molds the next day. Chilling the batter in this way is what allows the madeleines to develop the famous bump in the center.

☀ When ready to bake, preheat the oven to 325°F/160°C and bake for 17 minutes, or until golden (210°F/100°C) on an instant-read thermometer.

Financiers Nature

ALMOND CAKES

★★★
**MAKES ABOUT 12
INDIVIDUAL FINANCIERS
OR 36 MINI FINANCIERS
(SEE NOTE)**

PREPARATION TIME: 10 minutes
COOKING TIME: 10 to 15 minutes (depending on size)

- ½ stick plus 1¾ tsp (2⅓ oz/65 g) unsalted butter
- 1 cup plus 2 tbsp plus 1 tsp (4 oz/115 g) confectioners' sugar, sifted
- ⅓ cup plus 1 tsp (1¼ oz/35 g) all-purpose flour
- ⅓ cup plus 1 tbsp (2 oz/55 g) almond flour
- 1/16 tsp (0.6 g) baking powder
- 2 large (2⅛ oz/60 g) egg whites
- 1 tsp (5 mL) pure vanilla extract

Note: Classic financier molds measure 3¾ in (9.5 cm) by 2 in (5 cm), or 3 in (7.5 cm) round. Mini financiers are traditionally made in 1⅛-in (3-cm) semi-sphere silicone molds.

* Preheat the oven to 350°F/160°C. Grease the molds (do not grease them if you are using silicone molds).

* Melt the butter in a small saucepan or in a microwave-safe bowl.

* In a large bowl, whisk together the confectioners' sugar, all-purpose flour, almond flour, and baking powder.

* In a large mixing bowl or in the bowl of a standing mixer fitted with the whisk attachment, beat the egg whites on low speed while adding the flour mixture a little at a time, just until incorporated. Add the vanilla and the melted butter and beat until the batter is smooth.

* Fill the molds with the batter and bake for 15 minutes (10 minutes for minis), or until golden.

Financiers
Chocolat ou Pistache

CHOCOLATE OR PISTACHIO ALMOND CAKES

★ ★ ★
**MAKES ABOUT 12
INDIVIDUAL FINANCIERS
OR 36 MINI FINANCIERS
(SEE NOTE, PAGE 36)**

PREPARATION TIME: 10 minutes · COOKING TIME: 15 minutes
1 financier mold

Chocolate Almond Cakes

3 tbsp plus 2 ¾ tsp (2 oz/55 g) unsalted butter · 1 cup plus 2 tbsp plus 1 tsp (4 oz/115 g) confectioners' sugar, sifted · 2 ½ tbsp (½ oz/15 g) all-purpose flour · 3 tbsp plus 1 tsp (1 oz/30 g) almond flour · ¼ cup plus 1 tbsp (1 oz/30 g) hazelnut flour · ¹⁄₁₆ tsp (0.6 g) baking powder · 3 tbsp (½ oz/15 g) unsweetened Dutch-process cocoa powder, sifted · 2 large (2 ⅛ oz/60 g) egg whites

★ Follow the steps for the Financiers Nature on page 36, whisking together all of the dry ingredients.

You can sprinkle the financiers with chocolate chips prior to baking them.

Pistachio Almond Cakes

½ oz (12 g) pistachio paste · ½ stick plus 1 ¾ tsp (2 ⅓ oz/65 g) unsalted butter · 1 cup plus 2 tbsp plus 1 tsp (4 oz/115 g) confectioners' sugar, sifted · ⅓ cup plus 1 tsp (1 ¼ oz/35 g) all-purpose flour · ⅓ cup plus 1 tbsp (2 oz/55 g) almond flour · ¹⁄₁₆ tsp (0.6 g) baking powder · 2 large (2 ⅛ oz/60 g) egg whites

★ Follow the steps for the Financiers Nature on page 36, whisking together all of the dry ingredients, then incorporating the pistachio paste with the dry ingredients.

You can sprinkle the financiers with chopped pistachios prior to baking them.

Financiers au Thé Vert

GREEN TEA ALMOND CAKES

★ ★ ★
**MAKES ABOUT 12
INDIVIDUAL FINANCIERS
OR 36 MINI FINANCIERS
(SEE NOTE, PAGE 36)**

PREPARATION TIME: 10 minutes · COOKING TIME: 15 minutes
1 financier mold

- ½ stick plus 1¾ tsp (2⅓ oz/65 g) unsalted butter
- 1 cup plus 2 tbsp plus 1 tsp (4 oz/115 g) confectioners' sugar, sifted
- ⅓ cup plus 1 tsp (1¼ oz/35 g) all-purpose flour
- ⅓ cup plus 1 tbsp (2 oz/55 g) almond flour
- 1/16 tsp (0.6 g) baking powder
- 2 tsp (⅛ oz/4 g) matcha green tea powder
- 2 large (2⅛ oz/60 g) egg whites
- 2 tsp (¼ oz/6 g) poppy seeds

✳ Follow the steps for the Financiers Nature on page 36, whisking together all of the dry ingredients.

✳ Sprinkle the financiers with poppy seeds prior to baking them.

Tuiles aux Amandes

ALMOND WAFERS

★ ★ ★

MAKES
36 to 48
TUILES

PREPARATION TIME: 10 minutes • COOKING TIME: 7 minutes

- 3 large (3⅛ oz/90 g) egg whites
- ½ cup plus 2 tbsp (4½ oz/125 g) granulated sugar
- 1 tsp (5 mL) pure vanilla extract
- ¼ cup plus ½ tsp (1 oz/25 g) all-purpose flour
- 1 cup (4½ oz/125 g) slivered almonds

Variation: For Tuiles à l'Orange/Orange Wafers, replace the slivered almonds with chopped almonds and fold in 1¾ oz (50 g) finely diced candied orange peel with the almonds.

* Preheat the oven to 350°F/180°C. Line a baking sheet with parchment paper (or a silicone baking mat). Have ready rolling pins or glass bottles on which to cool the cookies.

* In a large mixing bowl, whisk together the egg whites, sugar, vanilla, and flour until smooth. Fold in the almonds using a silicone spatula.

* Drop the batter in rounded tablespoons onto the prepared baking sheet, at least 2 in (5 cm) apart.

* Bake for 7 minutes; the cookies should just begin to brown around the edges.

* As soon as they come out of the oven, transfer them from the baking sheet using a metal spatula and place them in groups of three to four on rolling pins or empty glass bottles so that they set slightly curved when cooled. As soon as they are cooled and firm, place them in an airtight container.

Palets aux Raisins

RAISIN CRISPS

★ ★ ★

MAKES ABOUT
36 to 48
COOKIES

PREPARATION TIME: 10 minutes · COOKING TIME: 7 minutes

- 3 large (3 ⅛ oz/90 g) egg whites
- ½ cup plus 2 tbsp (4 ½ oz/125 g) granulated sugar
- ¼ cup plus ½ tsp (1 oz/25 g) all-purpose flour
- ⅔ cup (4 ½ oz/125 g) almonds, finely chopped
- ¼ cup plus 2 tbsp (1 ¾ oz/50 g) raisins

✳ Preheat the oven to 350°F/180°C. Line a baking sheet with parchment paper (or a silicone baking mat).

✳ In a large bowl, whisk together the egg whites, sugar, and flour until smooth. Fold in the almonds using a silicone spatula.

✳ Drop the batter in rounded tablespoons onto the prepared baking sheet at least 2 in (5 cm) apart. Distribute the raisins on top and bake for 7 minutes; the cookies should just begin to brown around the edges.

✳ As soon as they come out of the oven, transfer them from the baking sheet to a wire rack using a metal spatula. When completely cooled, place them in an airtight container.

Diamants Nature
Diamants au Chocolat

BUTTER COOKIES OR CHOCOLATE BUTTER COOKIES

**MAKES ABOUT
60
DIAMANTS**

PREPARATION TIME: 15 minutes (over 2 days) · REFRIGERATION TIME: Overnight
COOKING TIME: 10 minutes

Butter Cookies

FOR THE DOUGH: 2 sticks (8 oz/225 g) unsalted butter, room temperature · ½ cup (3 ½ oz/100 g) granulated sugar · 1 tsp (5 mL) pure vanilla extract · 1 large (⅔ oz/19 g) egg yolk · 3 cups plus 3 tbsp (11 ⅛ oz/315 g) all-purpose flour

FOR FINISHING: 1 large (⅔ oz/19 g) egg yolk, beaten · ¼ cup plus 2 tbsp (2 ½ oz/75 g) granulated sugar

* The day before baking, make the dough. In the bowl of a standing mixer fitted with the paddle attachment, beat the butter with the sugar and vanilla until creamy. Add the egg yolk and flour and beat just until combined.

* Divide the dough into two equal portions, then roll them into 1½-in (4-cm)-thick logs. Wrap the logs in plastic wrap and refrigerate overnight.

* When ready to bake, preheat the oven to 350°F/180°C. Line a baking sheet with parchment paper (or a silicone baking mat).

* Unwrap the dough logs, then brush them with the egg yolk using a pastry brush. Roll the logs in the sugar, then cut them into ½-in (1.5-cm) slices.

* Place the cookies on the prepared baking sheet and bake for 10 minutes, or until golden. Transfer to a wire rack to cool.

Variation: Diamants au Chocolat: 2⅔ cups (9 ⅓ oz/265 g) all-purpose flour · ¼ cup plus 2 ½ tbsp (1 ¼ oz/35 g) unsweetened cocoa powder · 2 pinches salt · 2 sticks plus 2 tbsp plus 2 tsp (9 ⅓ oz/265 g) unsalted butter, room temperature · ½ cup plus 1 ¼ tsp (3 ⅔ oz/105 g) granulated sugar · 1 large (⅔ oz/19 g) egg yolk

Meringues

★ ★ ★

MAKES ABOUT
24
MEDIUM MERINGUES

PREPARATION TIME: 5 minutes · COOKING TIME: 1 hour

3 large (3 ⅛ oz/90 g) egg whites · 1 cup (7 oz/200 g) granulated sugar

∗ Preheat the oven to 210°F/100°C. Line a baking sheet with parchment paper (or a silicone baking mat).

∗ Beat the egg whites into stiff peaks; halfway through the beating time, start adding the sugar a little at a time. Drop the meringues by rounded tablespoons onto the prepared baking sheet at least 2 in (5 cm) apart. Bake for 1 hour.

∗ Let the meringues cool for several minutes on the parchment paper before removing them. Store them in an airtight container, especially if the air in the room is humid.

Variations: You can make colorful meringues by adding several drops of liquid food color or a small pinch of powdered food color of your choice to the egg whites while they are beating. Sprinkle some of them with sliced almonds before baking.

Langues-de-Chat

CRISPY "CAT TONGUE" COOKIES

★ ★ ★

MAKES ABOUT
72
COOKIES

PREPARATION TIME: 10 minutes • COOKING TIME: 5 minutes

½ stick plus 1 tbsp plus 1 tsp (2 ½ oz/75 g) unsalted butter, room temperature • 1¼ cups (4 ½ oz/125 g) confectioners' sugar, sifted • 3 large (3 ⅛ oz/90 g) egg whites • 1 cup (3 ½ oz/100 g) all-purpose flour • 1 tsp (5 mL) pure vanilla extract

∗ Preheat the oven to 350°F/180°C. Line a baking sheet with parchment paper (or a silicone baking mat).

∗ In a large mixing bowl or in the bowl of a standing mixer fitted with the paddle attachment, beat together the butter and confectioners' sugar until creamy. Beat in the egg whites, then the flour and vanilla, just until combined.

∗ Transfer the dough to a pastry bag fitted with a ¼-in (6-mm) plain pastry tube and pipe the batter into 2 ¼-in (6-cm) to 2 ¾-in (7-cm) "tongues" spaced ¾ in (2 cm) apart. Bake for 5 minutes. The cookies should just begin to brown around the edges.

∗ As soon as they come out of the oven, transfer them from the baking sheet to a wire rack using a metal spatula. When completely cooled, store them in an airtight container.

Cookies

DARK CHOCOLATE–NUT OR
WHITE CHOCOLATE–MACADAMIA COOKIES

★★★
MAKES ABOUT
24
COOKIES (SEE NOTE)

PREPARATION TIME: 10 minutes · FREEZING TIME: 1 hour · COOKING TIME: 14 to 18 minutes

FOR THE DARK CHOCOLATE COOKIES: 3 ½ cups plus 3 tbsp (13 oz/365 g) all-purpose flour · 2 ½ tsp (⅓ oz/10 g) baking powder · 1 tsp (¼ oz/6 g) salt · 1½ sticks plus 2 tsp (6 ½ oz/185 g) unsalted butter, room temperature · 2 cups minus 3 tbsp (14 oz/395 g) light brown sugar · 2 large (3 ½ oz/100 g) eggs · 12 oz (340 g) dark chocolate, in chips or evenly chopped · 1 cup (3 ½ oz/100 g) walnut halves · ¾ cup (3 ¾ oz/110 g) pecan halves

FOR THE WHITE CHOCOLATE COOKIES: 3 ¾ cups (13 oz/370 g) all-purpose flour · 2 ½ tsp (⅓ oz/10 g) baking powder · 1 tsp (¼ oz/6 g) salt · 1 ½ sticks plus 2 tsp (6 ½ oz/185 g) unsalted butter, room temperature · 1 ½ cups (12 oz/340 g) light brown sugar · 2 large (3 ½ oz/100 g) eggs · 12 oz (340 g) white chocolate, in chips or evenly chopped · ¾ cup (3 ½ oz/100 g) macadamia nuts · ¾ cup (3 ¾ oz/110 g) pecan halves

* Sift together the flour, baking powder, and salt. In the bowl of a standing mixer fitted with the paddle attachment, beat the butter and brown sugar until smooth and creamy. Then beat in the eggs, one at a time, until combined. Add the flour mixture and gently beat just until incorporated. Fold in the chocolate and nuts using a silicone spatula.
* Turn the dough out onto a large piece of plastic wrap and shape it into a log 2 in (5 cm) thick. Place the dough log in the freezer for at least 1 hour.
* When ready to bake, preheat the oven to 350°F/180°C. Line a baking sheet with parchment paper (or a silicone baking mat).
* Unwrap the chilled dough and cut it into ½-in (1.5-cm) slices. Place the slices on the prepared baking sheet at least 2 in (5 cm) apart and bake for 14 to 18 minutes; they should be dry around the edges but still moist in the center.
* Let the cookies cool slightly on the baking sheet before transferring them to a wire rack.

Serving Suggestion: Place the cookies in a microwave for 10 seconds to slightly melt the chocolate before enjoying them with a large glass of milk.

Note: You can double or triple this recipe and freeze the extra dough logs. Let the dough thaw slightly before slicing off as many cookies at a time as you wish to bake.

Pain Turc

ALMOND BISCUITS

★ ★ ★
MAKES ABOUT
100
COOKIES

PREPARATION TIME: 20 minutes (over 2 days) · REFRIGERATION TIME: Overnight
COOKING TIME: 6 minutes

1¾ sticks (7 oz/200 g) unsalted butter, room temperature · 1½ cups (5¼ oz/150 g) confectioners' sugar, sifted · 1 large (1 oz/30 g) egg white · 2½ cups (9 oz/250 g) all-purpose flour · 1½ cups (6⅛ oz/175 g) slivered almonds · ½ tsp (1 g) ground cinnamon

* The day before baking, make the dough. In the bowl of a standing mixer fitted with the paddle attachment, beat together the butter and confectioners' sugar until creamy. In a separate bowl, whisk together the egg white, flour, almonds, and cinnamon. Add this mixture to the butter mixture and beat just until it comes together into a smooth mass.
* Transfer the dough to a plastic food container measuring about 4 in (10 cm) by 6 in (16 cm), then press it down to a height of about 1⅓ in (3.5 cm). Refrigerate for 24 hours.
* When ready to bake, preheat the oven to 350°F/180°C. Line a baking sheet with parchment paper (or a silicone baking mat).
* Unmold the chilled block of dough onto a cutting board and cut it into 1½-in-(4-cm)-wide strips using a large knife. Cut each strip into ¼-in (5-mm) slices and transfer them to the prepared baking sheet spaced at least 1 in (2.5 cm) apart. Bake for 6 minutes.
* Let the cookies cool completely, then transfer them to an airtight container.

Les Tartes

TARTS

Pâte Sablée

BASIC CRUMBLY SWEET PASTRY DOUGH

★ ★ ★
**ONE ROUND TART PAN
BETWEEN 9 IN (22 CM)
AND 10 IN (25 CM) IN
DIAMETER**

PREPARATION TIME: 10 minutes (over 2 days) • REFRIGERATION TIME: 2 hours minimum, ideally overnight
COOKING TIME: Varies per recipe

¾ stick plus 1 tsp (3 ⅛ oz/90 g) unsalted butter, room temperature • 1 tbsp plus 1¾ tsp (¾ oz/20 g) granulated sugar • ⅓ cup plus 1 tsp (1¼ oz/35 g) confectioners' sugar, sifted • 2 pinches salt • 2 tbsp plus 1 tsp (¾ oz/20 g) almond flour • 1 large (1¾ oz/50 g) egg • 1½ cups minus 1 tsp (5 ⅛ oz/145 g) all-purpose flour

* The day before baking, make the dough. In the bowl of a standing mixer fitted with the paddle attachment, add the butter, granulated sugar, confectioners' sugar, salt, and almond flour (1).

* Beat on low speed, just until well blended (2). Add the egg and mix just until incorporated.

* Add the flour and mix just until incorporated. (You can also use a handheld mixer.)

* Wrap the dough in plastic wrap and let chill for at least 1 hour or ideally overnight (3).

* When ready to bake, prepare the crust. Preheat the oven (according to the recipe you use). On a lightly floured work surface, roll the dough into a ⅛-in (3-mm)-thick disk (4).

* To line the pan, fold the dough into fourths (5), center the point in the pan, then unfold it. Alternatively, roll the dough loosely around a rolling pin and unroll it, centered, draping it into the pan. Carefully fit the dough into the pan without stretching it and press it gently against the sides and into the corners; this will help prevent shrinking during baking. Trim the excess dough from around the edges (6) then refrigerate for 1 hour.

* Cut out a circle of parchment paper large enough to extend beyond the edges of the pan (7).

* Place it centered over the top of the chilled pan and press it down gently into the pan.

* Pour ceramic pie weights on the paper and spread them out evenly (8).

* Bake for the time specified in your recipe, then remove the tart from the oven and carefully lift out the pie weights using the edges of the parchment paper (9).

The tart shell can be filled with cream (such as almond cream) and fruit and baked again (refer to your recipe).

Tarte aux Fraises et Crème Légère à la Vanille

STRAWBERRY TART WITH VANILLA CREAM

★★★

SERVES
6 to 8

PREPARATION TIME: 30 minutes (not including the dough) · COOKING TIME: 25 minutes · REFRIGERATION TIME: 2 hours
One 9-in (22-cm) round removable-bottom tart pan or tart ring, or eight 4-in (10-cm) tart pans

FOR THE DOUGH: See the recipe on page 62
FOR THE ALMOND CREAM: · 3 tbsp plus 1¾ tsp (1¾ oz/50 g) unsalted butter, room temperature · ¼ cup (1¾ oz/50 g) granulated sugar · 1 large (1¾ oz/50 g) egg · ⅓ cup plus 1 tsp (1¾ oz/50 g) almond flour · 1 tsp (1/10 oz/3 g) cornstarch · 1 tsp (5 mL) rum
FOR THE VANILLA CRÈME LÉGÈRE: 2 large (1⅓ oz/38 g) egg yolks · ¼ cup plus 2½ tsp (2⅛ oz/60 g) granulated sugar · 2 tbsp plus 2 tsp (1 oz/25 g) cornstarch · 1 pinch vanilla powder, or ¼ tsp (2 mL) pure vanilla extract · 1⅓ cups (300 mL) whole milk · 1 (1/10 oz/3 g) gelatin sheet, or 1 tsp (1/10 oz/3 g) powdered gelatin · 2 tbsp (30 mL) very warm water · ⅔ cup (150 mL) heavy whipping cream, well chilled
FOR THE TOPPING: 1⅛ lb (500 g) fresh strawberries, hulled · Confectioners' sugar, for dusting

❋ The day before baking, make the dough. Let the dough chill for at least 1 hour or ideally overnight.

❋ When ready to bake, preheat the oven to 325°F/160°C. Line the pan or ring with the dough.

❋ Make the almond cream. In the bowl of a standing mixer fitted with the paddle attachment, beat the butter with the sugar until light-colored and creamy. Add the egg, almond flour, cornstarch, and rum, beating just until combined after each addition.

❋ Spread the almond cream evenly over the bottom of the crust. Bake for 20 minutes. Set aside to cool.

❋ Meanwhile, rinse the strawberries under cold water, then pat them dry on paper towels.

❋ Cut large strawberries in half.

❋ Make the vanilla crème légère. In a medium bowl, vigorously whisk together the egg yolks and sugar until light-colored. Whisk in the cornstarch and vanilla powder. In a heavy saucepan, warm the milk, then slowly pour it over the egg mixture, whisking constantly. Pour the combined mixture back into the saucepan and cook over medium heat, stirring constantly, until very thick, about 5 minutes.

❋ Soak the gelatin sheet for 10 minutes in a bowl of cold water. (If using powdered gelatin, sprinkle it over 1 tbsp plus 2 tsp (25 mL) cold water and stir to moisten it; let soften for 5 minutes.) Squeeze the water from the gelatin sheet and add it to the warm water; stir to dissolve. Incorporate the gelatin mixture into the warm custard. (If using powdered gelatin, stir in the softened gelatin until fully melted.) Scrape the mixture into a large bowl. Cool completely.

❋ Whip the chilled cream into soft peaks, then gently fold it into the custard mixture using a silicone spatula.

❋ Spread the crème légère evenly over the baked almond cream. Place the strawberries on top. Refrigerate for at least 2 hours. Dust the top with confectioners' sugar.

Tarte Chocolat Praline

CHOCOLATE PRALINE TART

SERVES
6 to 8

PREPARATION TIME: 30 minutes (not including the dough)
COOKING TIME: 45 minutes · REFRIGERATION TIME: 2 hours
One 8-in (20-cm) round removable-bottom tart pan or tart ring, or eight 4-in (10-cm) tart pans

FOR THE DOUGH: See the recipe on page 62
FOR THE CHOCOLATE FILLING: 3 ¾ oz (110 g) dark chocolate, in disks or evenly chopped · 3 ¾ oz (110 g) milk chocolate, in disks or evenly chopped · ¾ cup plus 1½ tbsp (200 mL) heavy whipping cream · 3 tbsp plus ½ tsp (1½ oz/45 g) unsalted butter · 2 large (3 ½ oz/100 g) eggs · 1 large (²⁄₃ oz/19 g) egg yolk · 1 tbsp (15 mL) pure vanilla extract
FOR THE PRALINE FEUILLETINE: 6 ⅓ oz (180 g) praline paste · ¾ oz (20 g) feuilletine or crushed lace cookies (florentines)
FOR THE GLAZE: 2 ½ oz (75 g) dark chocolate, in disks or evenly chopped · 1 tbsp plus 2 tsp (1 oz/25 g) unsalted butter

* The day before baking, make the dough. Let the dough chill for at least 1 hour or ideally overnight.

* When ready to bake, preheat the oven to 325°F/160°C. Line the pan with the dough and prebake it for 15 minutes.

* Make the chocolate filling. Place the dark and milk chocolate together in a large bowl. In a heavy saucepan, bring the cream to a boil with the butter and pour it over the chocolate. Let rest for several minutes and whisk until smooth. In a small bowl, whisk together the eggs, egg yolk, and vanilla. Add this mixture to the chocolate mixture and whisk until smooth.

* Make the praline feuilletine. Mix together the praline paste and the feuilletine then spread this mixture out over the bottom of the prebaked crust.

* Pour the chocolate filling over the praline mixture and spread it out evenly. Bake for 30 minutes. Cool completely. Refrigerate for at least 2 hours.

* Make the glaze. In a large heatproof bowl set over a pot of simmering water, melt the chocolate and the butter together (or place them in a microwave-safe bowl and microwave for 1 minute), then stir until completely melted. Carefully pour the warm glaze over the top of the tart in a thin layer.

You can decorate the tart with several large pieces of nougatine, or about 3 ½ tbsp (1 oz/30 g) of hazelnuts that have been lightly browned in a nonstick frying pan with 2 tbsp plus 1¼ tsp (1 oz/30 g) granulated sugar. Let the hazelnuts cool on a piece of parchment paper before placing them on the tart.

Tarte aux Abricots et Crème Amande-Pistache

APRICOT-PISTACHIO TART

SERVES
6 to 8

PREPARATION TIME: 20 minutes (not including the dough) · COOKING TIME: 45 minutes

One 8-in (20-cm) round removable-bottom tart pan or tart ring, or eight 4-in (10-cm) tart pans

FOR THE DOUGH: See the recipe on page 62

FOR THE ALMOND-PISTACHIO CREAM: ½ stick plus 1 tbsp plus 1 tsp (2½ oz/75 g) unsalted butter, room temperature · 1½ oz (40 g) pistachio paste · ¼ cup plus 2 tbsp (2½ oz/75 g) granulated sugar · 2 large (3½ oz/100 g) eggs · ½ cup plus 2 tsp (2½ oz/75 g) almond flour · 1 tbsp (⅓ oz/10 g) cornstarch · 2 tsp (10 mL) rum

FOR THE TOPPING: 1¾ lb (800 g) preserved apricot halves, or 2¼ lb (1 kg) fresh apricots

FOR THE GLAZE: 3 tbsp (45 mL) neutral glaze, or 2 tbsp (1½ oz/43 g) apricot preserves diluted with 2 tbsp (30 mL) water and strained · 3 tbsp (1 oz/30 g) pistachios, chopped

* The day before baking, make the dough. Let the dough chill for at least 1 hour or ideally overnight.

* When ready to bake, preheat the oven to 325°F/160°C. Line the pan with the dough and prebake it for 15 minutes.

* Make the almond-pistachio cream. In the bowl of a standing mixer fitted with the paddle attachment, beat the butter, pistachio paste, and sugar until creamy. Add the eggs, almond flour, cornstarch, and rum, beating just until combined after each addition. Spread the cream evenly into the prebaked crust. Place the apricots on their edges on top of the cream in a rosette pattern and bake for 30 minutes.

* Warm the neutral glaze and let it cool. Brush it over the top of the tart using a pastry brush. Sprinkle with chopped pistachios.

Tarte au Citron Meringuée
LEMON MERINGUE TART

★★★

SERVES
6 to 8

PREPARATION TIME: 25 minutes (not including the dough)
COOKING TIME: 25 to 26 minutes • REFRIGERATION TIME: 2 hours
One 9-in (23-cm) round removable-bottom tart pan or tart ring, or eight 4-in (10-cm) tart pans

FOR THE DOUGH: See the recipe on page 62
FOR THE LEMON CREAM: 2 large (3 ½ oz/100 g) eggs • ¾ cup plus 1 tbsp plus ½ tsp (5 ¾ oz/165 g) granulated sugar • ¼ cup plus 3 tbsp minus ½ tsp (2 ⅓ oz/65 g) cornstarch • 1 ½ cups (350 mL) freshly squeezed lemon juice, preferably with the pulp (from 8 or 9 lemons) • ¾ stick plus 1 tsp (3 ⅛ oz/90 g) unsalted butter, cut into pieces
FOR THE MERINGUE: 2 large (2 ⅛ oz/60 g) egg whites • ½ cup plus 1 tbsp plus 1 ¾ tsp (4 ¼ oz/120 g) granulated sugar

* The day before baking, make the dough. Let the dough chill for at least 1 hour or ideally overnight.
* When ready to bake, preheat the oven to 325°F/160°C. Line the pan with the dough and prebake it for 24 minutes.
* Make the lemon cream. In a medium bowl, whisk together the eggs, sugar, and cornstarch. In a heavy saucepan, bring the lemon juice to a boil. Whisk in the egg mixture. Bring the mixture to a boil and cook for 2 minutes, stirring constantly, until very thick. Let cool. Add the butter pieces to the cream. Using an immersion blender, blend the mixture until smooth and the butter is incorporated. Scrape the lemon cream into the prebaked crust and spread it out evenly. Refrigerate for at least 2 hours.
* Make the meringue. Place the egg whites in the bowl of a standing mixer. In a small heavy saucepan, heat the sugar and 2 tbsp (30 mL) water over high heat to 250°F/121°C. (If you do not have a candy thermometer, drop a small quantity of the hot syrup into a bowl of cold water. It should form a ball and feel soft when pinched between your fingers.)
* Meanwhile, beat the egg whites until soft peaks form. When the syrup reaches 250°F/121°C, pour it in a steady stream down the inside edge of the bowl while beating constantly, just until the whites are stiff and glossy. Using a pastry bag or a silicone spatula, pipe or spread the meringue on top of the tart. Lightly brown the meringue using a miniature torch, or place it under the broiler for 1 to 2 minutes with the oven door partially open, watching it carefully.

Tarte Passion-Framboises

PASSION FRUIT AND RASPBERRY TART

★ ★ ★

SERVES
6 to 8

PREPARATION TIME: 20 minutes (not including the dough) · COOKING TIME: 29 minutes
FREEZING TIME: 1 hour
One 9-in (23-cm) round removable-bottom tart pan or a tart ring, or eight 4-in (10-cm) tart pans

FOR THE DOUGH: See the recipe on page 62
FOR THE PASSION FRUIT CREAM: ½ cup (4 oz/110 g) store-bought passion fruit purée, or the juice and pulp from about 6 fresh passion fruits (see Note) · 1 tbsp (15 mL) freshly squeezed lemon juice (from ½ lemon) · 3 large (5¼ oz/150 g) eggs · ½ cup plus 2 tbsp (4½ oz/125 g) granulated sugar · 1½ (⅛ oz/5 g) gelatin sheets, or 1½ tsp (⅛ oz/5 g) powdered gelatin · 2 sticks plus 2 tsp (8½ oz/240 g) unsalted butter, chilled and cut into pieces
FOR THE GLAZE (OPTIONAL): 2 tbsp (30 mL) neutral glaze, or 2 tbsp (1½ oz/43 g) apricot preserves diluted with 2 tbsp (30 mL) water and strained · 1 tbsp (½ oz/14 g) store-bought passion fruit purée
FOR THE DECORATION: 1 pint (8 oz/226 g) fresh raspberries

* The day before baking, make the dough. Let the dough chill for at least 1 hour or ideally overnight.

* When ready to bake, preheat the oven to 325°F/160°C. Line the pan with the dough and prebake it for 24 minutes.

* Make the passion fruit cream. If using fresh passion fruit, strain the juice and pulp over a bowl through a fine-mesh strainer to remove the seeds; measure out ½ cup (3¾ oz/110 g) of the juice and pulp.

* In a heavy saucepan, whisk together the passion fruit purée, lemon juice, eggs, and sugar.

* Cook over gentle heat for about 5 minutes while whisking constantly, just until thick; do not allow it to boil.

* Soak the gelatin sheets for 10 minutes in a bowl of cold water. (If using powdered gelatin, sprinkle it over 2½ tbsp (40 mL) cold water and stir it to moisten; let soften for

5 minutes.) Squeeze the water from the gelatin sheets and add them to the saucepan (or add the softened powdered gelatin, if using); stir to dissolve. Cool slightly. Add the butter pieces to the cream. Using an immersion blender, blend the mixture until smooth and the butter is incorporated.

* When completely cooled, scrape the cream into the prebaked crust and spread it out evenly. Freeze for at least 1 hour.

* Make the glaze, if using. In a saucepan, warm the neutral glaze with the passion fruit purée. Pour the mixture on top of the chilled tart and spread to cover.

* Place the raspberries on top for decoration. You can also dry several passion fruit seeds then distribute a few on top of the glaze.

Store-bought passion fruit purée will be much more economical than using fresh fruit.

FIG AND PEAR TART

SERVES
6 to 8

PREPARATION TIME: 20 minutes (not including the dough) · COOKING TIME: 30 minutes
One 9-in (23-cm) round removable-bottom tart pan or a tart ring, or eight 4-in (10-cm) tart pans

FOR THE DOUGH:

• See the recipe on page 62

FOR THE ALMOND-PISTACHIO CREAM:

• 1 stick minus 1 tbsp (3 ½ oz/100 g) unsalted butter, room temperature
• ⅓ oz (10 g) pistachio paste
• ½ cup (3 ½ oz/100 g) granulated sugar
• 2 large (3 ½ oz/100 g) eggs
• ¾ cup minus 1 ½ tsp (3 ½ oz/100 g) almond flour
• 1 tbsp (⅓ oz/10 g) cornstarch

FOR THE TOPPING:

• 14 oz (400 g) pear halves in syrup, halved, or 4 fresh pears, peeled and sliced
• 9 oz (250 g) fresh figs, quartered
• 3 tbsp (45 mL) neutral glaze
or 2 tbsp (1 ½ oz/43 g) apricot preserves diluted with 2 tbsp (30 mL) water and strained (optional)

✳ The day before baking, make the dough. Let the dough chill for at least 1 hour or ideally overnight.

✳ When ready to bake, preheat the oven to 340°F/170°C. Line the pan with the dough.

✳ Make the almond-pistachio cream. In the bowl of a standing mixer fitted with the paddle attachment, beat the butter, pistachio paste, and sugar until creamy. Add the eggs, almond flour, and cornstarch, beating just until combined after each addition. Spread the cream evenly into the crust. Place the fruit on top of the cream in a rosette pattern and bake for 30 minutes.

✳ Warm the glaze, if using, then brush it over the top of the tart using a pastry brush.

Tarte Monge
MIXED BERRY TART

★ ★ ★

SERVES
6 to 8

PREPARATION TIME: 25 minutes (not including the dough) · FREEZING TIME: Overnight
COOKING TIME: 24 minutes · REFRIGERATION TIME: 3 hours
One 9-in (23-cm) round removable-bottom tart pan or a tart ring, or eight 4-in (10-cm) tart pans

FOR THE DOUGH: See the recipe on page 62
FOR THE FRUIT DISK: 14 oz (400 g) mixed red fruits (such as raspberries, red currants, blueberries, blackberries), fresh or frozen · ¼ cup plus 2 ½ tsp (2 ⅛ oz/60 g) granulated sugar · 3 (⅓ oz/9 g) gelatin sheets, or 1 tbsp (⅓ oz/9 g) powdered gelatin · ⅓ cup (3 oz/80 g) store-bought raspberry purée
FOR THE FROMAGE BLANC CREAM: 7 oz (200 g) fromage blanc (see Note) · ½ cup plus 1 tbsp plus 2 tsp (2 ⅛ oz/60 g) confectioners' sugar, sifted · 1 tbsp (15 mL) kirsch (cherry liqueur) · 2 (¼ oz/6 g) gelatin sheets, or 2 tsp (¼ oz/6 g) powdered gelatin · 2 tbsp (30 mL) very warm water · ¾ cup plus 1½ tbsp (200 mL) heavy whipping cream, well chilled

✳ The day before baking, make the dough. Let the dough chill for at least 1 hour or ideally overnight.

✳ Make the fruit disk. If using fresh fruit, rinse it briefly (except raspberries and blackberries) and place on paper towels to dry. In a small saucepan, whisk together the sugar and ¼ cup (60 mL) water and heat, while stirring, until the sugar is dissolved and the mixture is hot.

✳ Soak the gelatin sheets for 10 minutes in a bowl of cold water. (If using powdered gelatin, sprinkle it over ¼ cup plus 1 tbsp (75 mL) cold water and stir to moisten it; let soften for 5 minutes.) Squeeze the water from the gelatin sheets and add them to the saucepan (or add the softened powdered gelatin, if using); stir to dissolve. Add the raspberry purée and stir to combine.

✳ Pour the purée mixture into a round silicone cake pan (or in a tart pan with a removable bottom, lined with plastic wrap) that is slightly smaller in diameter than the tart pan. Distribute the fruit on top and place the pan in the freezer until the next day.

✳ When ready to bake, preheat the oven to 325°F/160°C. Line the tart pan with the dough and prebake it for 24 minutes.

✳ Make the fromage blanc cream. In a large mixing bowl, whisk together the fromage blanc, confectioners' sugar, and kirsch. Soak the gelatin sheets for 10 minutes in a bowl of cold water. (If using powdered gelatin, sprinkle it over 3 tbsp plus 1 tsp (50 mL) cold water and stir to moisten it; let soften for 5 minutes.) Squeeze the water from the gelatin sheets and add them to the warm water; stir to dissolve (or gently melt the softened powdered gelatin, if using). Incorporate the gelatin a little at a time into the fromage blanc mixture while whisking vigorously. Whip the cream and fold it into the mixture using a silicone spatula.

✳ Assemble the tart. Spread the fromage blanc cream evenly into the prebaked crust. Carefully unmold the frozen fruit purée disk and place it on top of the cream. Refrigerate the tart for at least 3 hours to allow the filling to set and the fruit disk to thaw slowly.

Full-fat plain Greek yogurt or whole-milk ricotta may be used as a substitute for fromage blanc.

Tarte aux Framboises Façon Sablé Breton

RASPBERRY TART WITH SHORTBREAD CRUST

★ ★ ★

SERVES
6 to 8

PREPARATION TIME: 25 minutes · COOKING TIME: 15 minutes · REFRIGERATION TIME: 2 hours

One 9-in (23-cm) round removable-bottom tart pan or ring, or square cake ring

FOR THE CREAM BASE: 2 large (1⅓ oz/38 g) egg yolks · ¼ cup plus 2 tbsp (2½ oz/75 g) granulated sugar · 3 tbsp (1 oz/30 g) cornstarch · 1⅓ cups (300 mL) whole milk · 4 (½ oz/12 g) gelatin sheets, or 1 tbsp plus 1 tsp (½ oz/12 g) powdered gelatin · 2 tbsp (30 mL) very warm water · 3 tbsp plus ½ tsp (1½ oz/45 g) unsalted butter, cut into pieces · ⅔ cup (150 mL) heavy whipping cream, well chilled FOR THE SHORTBREAD PASTRY: 1 stick minus 1 tbsp (3½ oz/100 g) unsalted butter, room temperature · ¼ cup plus 3 tbsp plus ½ tsp (3⅛ oz/90 g) granulated sugar · 1⅓ cups plus 2 tsp (4¾ oz/135 g) all-purpose flour · ⅓ tsp (1/10 oz/2 g) salt · 1⅔ tsp (¼ oz/7 g) baking powder · 2 large (1⅓ oz/38 g) egg yolks FOR THE TOPPING: 2 pints (16 oz/452 g) fresh raspberries · 1 tbsp (15 mL) honey

* Make the cream base. In a medium bowl, vigorously whisk together the egg yolks and sugar just until lightened. Whisk in the cornstarch. In a saucepan, warm the milk and pour it slowly over the egg mixture while whisking constantly. Pour the entire mixture back into the saucepan and cook over medium heat, whisking constantly, until very thick, about 5 minutes.

* Soak the gelatin sheets for 10 minutes in a bowl of cold water. (If using powdered gelatin, sprinkle it over ¼ cup plus 2½ tbsp (100 mL) cold water and stir to moisten it; let soften for 5 minutes.) Squeeze the water from the gelatin sheets and add them to the warm water; stir to dissolve. Stir the gelatin mixture into the warm custard (or stir in the softened powdered gelatin, if using, until fully melted). Cool slightly. Add the butter pieces to the cream. Using an immersion blender, blend the custard until smooth and the

butter is incorporated. Cover the surface with plastic wrap and refrigerate.

* Preheat the oven to 340°F/170°C.

* Make the shortbread pastry. In the bowl of a standing mixer fitted with the paddle attachment, beat the butter, sugar, flour, salt, and baking powder on low speed, just until it has a sandy texture (you can also use a handheld mixer). Gently beat in the egg yolks, working the dough as little as possible.

* Line the tart ring with the dough, line with foil or parchment paper, and pour ceramic pie weights on the paper. Spread them out evenly and prebake it for 15 minutes. Cool completely. Remove the weights and ring.

* Assemble the tart. Whip the cream and fold it into the cream base using a silicone spatula. Spread the cream evenly over the prebaked crust and place the raspberries on top. Drizzle the honey on the top. Refrigerate for at least 2 hours.

Tarte Tatin

APPLE UPSIDE-DOWN TART

SERVES
6 to 8

PREPARATION TIME: 20 minutes (not including the dough) · COOKING TIME: 45 minutes
One 9-in (23-cm) round cake pan

8 medium baking apples (see Note) · 1½ cups (10 ½ oz/300 g) granulated sugar · 10 ½ oz (300 g)
all-butter puff pastry dough, homemade (see page 134) or store-bought, fresh or frozen

* Peel and quarter the apples.

* Preheat the oven to 350°F/175°C. In a small heavy saucepan, boil the sugar with ¼ cup (60 mL) water until caramelized. When the syrup has turned a dark reddish-brown color, pour it into the cake pan. Place the apples on their edges, very close together, on top of the caramel.

* Roll out the puff pastry dough into a circle that is slightly larger than the pan and place it on top of the apples, tucking it down to cover the edges of the apples. Bake for 45 minutes. Cool on a rack for 15 minutes before inverting it onto a serving plate.

Note: Be sure to purchase apples that are best for baking, such as Granny Smith, Baldwin, or Golden Delicious.

Tarte Crumble aux Griottes

CHERRY CRUMBLE TART

★ ★ ★

SERVES
6 to 8

PREPARATION TIME: 20 minutes (not including the dough) • COOKING TIME: 30 minutes • One 10-in (25-cm) round tart or cake pan, or eight 4-in (10-cm) tart pans

FOR THE DOUGH: See recipe on page 62
FOR THE ALMOND-PISTACHIO CREAM: 3 tbsp plus 1¾ tsp (1¾ oz/50 g) unsalted butter, room temperature • ⅓ oz (10 g) pistachio paste • ¼ cup (1¾ oz/50 g) granulated sugar • 1 large (1¾ oz/50 g) egg • ⅓ cup plus 1 tsp (1¾ oz/50 g) almond flour • ½ tbsp (⅛ oz/5 g) cornstarch
FOR THE CRUMBLE AND FRUIT TOPPING: 1 cup minus 1 tbsp (4½ oz/130 g) almond flour • ¼ cup plus 3 tbsp plus ½ tsp (3⅛ oz/90 g) granulated sugar • 1 tbsp (15 mL) Almond-Pistachio Cream (reserved) • 1½ lb (700 g) frozen Morello cherries

* The day before baking, make the dough. Let the dough chill for at least 1 hour or ideally overnight.
* When ready to bake, preheat the oven to 350°F/180°C. Line the pan with the dough.
* Make the almond-pistachio cream. In the bowl of a standing mixer fitted with the paddle attachment, beat the butter, pistachio paste, and sugar until creamy. Add the egg, almond flour, and cornstarch, beating just until combined after each addition. Spread the cream evenly into the crust. Reserve 1 tbsp (15 mL) of the cream for the crumble.
* Make the crumble. In a large bowl, mix together the almond flour, sugar, and the reserved almond-pistachio cream using your fingers, until the mixture has a sandy texture with large pieces.
* Spread the remaining almond-pistachio cream evenly into the pan and place the cherries on top of the cream-filled crust. Cover with the crumble and bake for 30 minutes.

Variation: For Tarte Crumble aux Pommes/Apple Crumble Tart, replace the cherries with 6 or 7 small apples, peeled and diced. In the almond-pistachio cream, replace the pistachio paste with 2 tbsp (30 mL) rum.

Tarte au Caramel et au Chocolat au Lait

MILK CHOCOLATE AND CARAMEL TART

★★★

SERVES
6 to 8

PREPARATION TIME: 25 minutes (not including the dough) · COOKING TIME: 24 minutes
FREEZING TIME: 1 hour · REFRIGERATION TIME: Overnight
One 8-in (20-cm) round removable-bottom tart pan or a cake ring, or eight 4-in (10-cm) tart pans

FOR THE DOUGH: See the recipe on page 62
FOR THE CARAMEL: ¼ cup plus 2 ½ tsp (2 ⅛ oz/60 g) granulated sugar plus 3 tbsp (2 ⅛ oz/60 g) glucose syrup (or corn syrup), or ½ cup plus 1 tbsp plus 1¾ tsp (4 ¼ oz/120 g) granulated sugar · ¼ cup (60 mL) heavy whipping cream · ⅓ tsp (1⁄10 oz/2 g) kosher salt · 1 tbsp plus 2 tsp (1 oz/25 g) unsalted butter
FOR THE MILK CHOCOLATE GANACHE: 5 ¼ oz (150 g) milk chocolate, in disks or evenly chopped · 1 cup plus 2 ¾ tsp (250 mL) heavy whipping cream
FOR THE DECORATION: Small caramels

* The day before baking, make the dough. Let the dough chill for at least 1 hour or ideally overnight.

* When ready to bake, preheat the oven to 325°F/160°C. Line the pan with the dough and prebake it for 24 minutes.

* Make the caramel. In a small heavy saucepan, heat the sugar, glucose syrup, and 2 tbsp (30 mL) water over high heat to 338°F/170°C to make a caramel that is medium-dark amber in color. Off the heat, carefully add the cream to the caramel while stirring constantly (be careful of splattering), then stir in the salt and butter. Place back on the heat.

Cook the caramel cream while stirring vigorously with a whisk to reduce it slightly, 2 or 3 minutes, until it reaches 221°F/105°C. Let cool slightly. Pour the caramel into the prebaked crust. Place in the freezer for at least 1 hour.

* Make the milk chocolate ganache. Place the chocolate in a large bowl. In a heavy saucepan, bring the cream to a boil and pour it over the chocolate. Let stand for several minutes, then whisk until smooth. When cooled slightly, pour the chocolate into the tart over the chilled caramel and refrigerate overnight. Decorate the tart with small caramels.

Tarte au Café et au Chocolat

COFFEE AND CHOCOLATE TART

SERVES
6 to 8

PREPARATION TIME: 20 minutes (not including the dough) · COOKING TIME: 54 minutes
REFRIGERATION TIME: 3 hours · One 8-in (20-cm) round removable-bottom tart pan or a tart ring,
one 7-in (18-cm) square ring, or eight 4-in (10-cm) tart pans

FOR THE DOUGH: See the recipe on page 62
FOR THE COFFEE SAUCE: 1 cup plus 2 ¾ tsp (250 mL) heavy whipping cream · 3 tbsp plus 1¾ tsp
(1¾ oz/50 g) unsalted butter · 1 tbsp (½ oz/13 g) instant coffee · ¼ cup (1¾ oz/50 g) granulated
sugar · 2 large (3½ oz/100 g) eggs · 2 large (1⅓ oz/38 g) egg yolks · 1½ tbsp (½ oz/15 g) cornstarch
FOR THE DARK CHOCOLATE GANACHE: 5½ oz (160 g) premium couverture dark chocolate, in disks or
evenly chopped · ¾ cup plus 1½ tbsp (200 mL) heavy whipping cream · 2 tbsp plus 1 tsp (1¼ oz/35 g)
unsalted butter · 2 tbsp plus 2½ tsp (1¼ oz/35 g) granulated sugar
FOR THE DECORATION: Chocolate-covered coffee beans or chocolate pieces

⁎ The day before baking, make the dough. Let the dough chill for at least 1 hour or ideally overnight.

⁎ When ready to bake, preheat the oven to 325°F/160°C. Line the pan with the dough and prebake it for 24 minutes.

⁎ Make the coffee sauce. In a heavy saucepan, heat the cream, butter, instant coffee, and sugar, and stir to combine. In a large bowl, whisk together the eggs, egg yolks, and cornstarch. Whisk the egg mixture into the cream mixture in the saucepan and stir to combine.

⁎ Pour the coffee sauce into the prebaked crust. Increase the oven temperature to 350°F/180°C and bake for 30 minutes. Place the tart on a wire rack to cool.

⁎ Make the dark chocolate ganache. Place the chocolate in a large mixing bowl. In a heavy saucepan, heat the cream, butter, and sugar and stir to combine. Pour the cream mixture over the chocolate. Let sit for several minutes, then stir with a whisk until smooth. Pour the ganache into the tart.

⁎ Refrigerate for at least 3 hours.

Decorate the tart with chocolate-covered coffee beans or chocolate pieces.

La Fameuse Pâte à Choux

CHOUX PASTRIES

Pâte à Choux

CLASSIC CREAM PUFF DOUGH

★ ★ ★

**MAKES 12 LARGE
CREAM PUFFS, 12 ÉCLAIRS,
8 PARIS-BREST, 4 TO 5
DOZEN CHOUQUETTES,
8 SAINT-HONORÉ,
OR 8 RELIGIEUSES**

PREPARATION TIME: 15 minutes • COOKING TIME: Varies per recipe

⅓ cup (80 mL) whole milk • 1 tsp (⅛ oz/4 g) granulated sugar • 1 stick plus 1 tsp (4 ¼ oz/120 g) unsalted butter • ½ tsp (1/10 oz/3 g) salt • 1⅔ cups minus 2 tsp (5 ½ oz/160 g) all-purpose flour, sifted • 3 large (5 ¼ oz/150 g) eggs

* Preheat the oven to 350°F/180°C. Line a baking sheet with parchment paper.

* In a heavy saucepan, combine the milk, sugar, butter, salt, and ⅓ cup (80 mL) water ①.

* Bring to a full boil, ② then add the flour all at once ③. Cook over low heat while stirring constantly with a wooden spoon until the dough pulls completely away from the sides of the pan ④.

* Remove from the heat. Let cool slightly, then vigorously stir in one egg using the wooden spoon ⑤. Add the remaining eggs one at a time while stirring vigorously ⑥.

* (Steps 4, 5, and 6 can also be performed in a standing mixer fitted with the paddle attachment.)

* Using a silicone spatula, transfer the dough to a pastry bag fitted with a ¼-in (10-mm) open star pastry tube.

FOR CREAM PUFFS:

* Pipe puffs 2 ¼ in (6 cm) in diameter, squeezing the bag while moving it with your wrist in a circular motion. Release the pressure from the bag and quickly pull the tip up to release it from the dough ⑦. Bake according to the time specified in the recipe.

FOR ÉCLAIRS:

* Pipe straight lines about 4 in (10 cm) long ⑧. Bake according to the time specified in the recipe.

FOR PARIS-BREST:

* Pipe rings about 4 in (10 cm) in diameter ⑨. Sprinkle them with sliced almonds ⑩. Bake according to the time specified in the recipe.

FOR CHOUQUETTES:

* Pipe puffs 1⅛ in (3 cm) to 1½ in (4 cm) in diameter ⑪.

* Sprinkle them with coarse sugar ⑫. Bake according to the time specified in the recipe.

FOR A SAINT-HONORÉ:

* Using a cake ring or an inverted plate, cut out a circle of puff pastry dough (for homemade puff pastry dough, see page 134) ⑬.

* Pipe a line of the cream puff dough around the edge of the puff pastry dough circle ⑭.

* Pipe small puffs using the remaining cream puff dough. Bake according to the time specified in the recipe.

Chouquettes

SUGAR PUFFS

PREPARATION TIME: 15 minutes • COOKING TIME: 25 minutes

- ¾ cup plus 1½ tbsp (200 mL) whole milk
- 1 tbsp (½ oz/13 g) granulated sugar
- 1½ sticks plus 1 tsp (6⅛ oz/175 g) unsalted butter
- ½ tsp (1⁄10 oz/3 g) salt
- 2⅓ cups (8⅛ oz/230 g) all-purpose flour, sifted
- ⅓ cup (3 oz/80 g) crème fraîche
- 6 large (10½ oz/300 g) eggs
- ½ cup (3½ oz/100 g) pearl sugar

* Preheat the oven to 400°F/200°C. Line a baking sheet with parchment paper.

* Make the dough for chouquettes following the step-by-step instructions on page 106. In a heavy saucepan, combine the milk, sugar, butter, salt, and ¾ cup plus 3 tbsp (220 mL) water and bring to a full boil. Add the flour all at once, and cook over low heat while stirring constantly with a wooden spoon until the dough pulls completely away from the sides of the pan.

* Remove from the heat. Let cool slightly, then stir in the crème fraîche. Vigorously stir in one egg using the wooden spoon. Add the remaining eggs one at a time, stirring vigorously after each addition.

* Using a silicone spatula, scrape the dough into a pastry bag fitted with a 5⁄16-in (8-mm) plain pastry tube. Pipe puffs 1⅛ in (3 cm) to 1½ in (4 cm) in diameter, squeezing the bag while moving it with your wrist in a circular motion. Release the pressure from the bag and quickly pull the tip up to release it from the dough.

* Sprinkle with the pearl sugar and bake for 25 minutes.

Paris-Brest

LAYERED PASTRY CAKE WITH PRALINE CREAM

★ ★ ★

**MAKES 8 INDIVIDUAL
PARIS-BREST (SEE
VARIATION)**

PREPARATION TIME: 30 minutes (over 2 days, not including the cream puff dough)
REFRIGERATION TIME: Overnight, plus 3 hours · COOKING TIME: 30 minutes

FOR THE PRALINE CREAM: 3 large (2 oz/57 g) egg yolks · ¼ cup plus 2 ½ tsp (2 ⅛ oz/60 g) granulated sugar · 3 tbsp (1 oz/30 g) cornstarch · 1 ⅓ cups (300 mL) whole milk · 3 tbsp plus 1 tsp (50 mL) heavy whipping cream · 3 (⅓ oz/9 g) gelatin sheets, or 1 tbsp (⅓ oz/9 g) powdered gelatin · 3 tbsp (45 mL) very warm water · 6 oz (170 g) praline paste · 1 stick plus 1 tbsp plus 2 tsp (5 oz/140 g) unsalted butter, room temperature
FOR THE CREAM PUFF DOUGH: See the recipe on page 106 · ¼ cup plus 2 tbsp (1 oz/30 g) sliced almonds
FOR THE CHANTILLY CREAM (OPTIONAL): ¾ cup plus 1 ½ tbsp (200 mL) heavy whipping cream · ¼ cup minus 2 tsp (¾ oz/20 g) confectioners' sugar, sifted

⁎ The day before baking, make the praline cream. In a medium bowl, vigorously whisk together the egg yolks and sugar just until lightened. Whisk in the cornstarch. In a saucepan, warm the milk with the cream then pour the milk mixture over the egg mixture while whisking constantly. Pour the entire mixture back into the saucepan and cook over medium heat, whisking constantly, until very thick, about 5 minutes.

⁎ Soak the gelatin sheets for 10 minutes in a bowl of cold water. (If using powdered gelatin, sprinkle it over ¼ cup plus 1 tbsp (75 mL) cold water and stir to moisten it; let soften for 5 minutes.) Squeeze the water from the gelatin sheets and add them to the warm water; stir to dissolve. Add the gelatin mixture to the warm custard (or stir in the softened powdered gelatin, if using, until fully melted) along with the praline paste and stir to combine. Let cool slightly.

⁎ Add the butter pieces to the cream. Using an immersion blender, blend the mixture until smooth and the butter is incorporated. Cover the surface with plastic wrap and refrigerate overnight.

⁎ When ready to bake, preheat the oven to 400°F/200°C. Line a baking sheet with parchment paper.

⁎ Make the cream puff dough. Make dough for Paris-Brest following the step-by-step instructions on page 106. Bake for 30 minutes. Cool completely.

⁎ Assemble the Paris-Brest. Slice the cream puff rings in half horizontally. In the bowl of a standing mixer fitted with the whisk attachment, beat the praline cream for several minutes on low speed to lighten it. Scrape it into a pastry bag fitted with an open star pastry tube. Fill the bottom halves of the pastry circles with the praline cream.

⁎ Make the chantilly cream, if using. Beat the cream to soft peaks, adding the confectioners' sugar halfway through the beating time. Using a separate pastry bag fitted with an open star pastry tube, pipe the chantilly cream on top of the praline cream. Replace the pastry tops. Refrigerate for at least 3 hours.

Variation: This recipe will also make one large Paris-Brest that serves 8 to 10. For a large Paris-Brest, there are two approaches: Pipe two adjoining circles of cream puff dough (one inside the other), then pipe a third circle on top of the groove between the first two circles. Alternatively, pipe eight perfectly round puffs on top of the groove.

Éclairs à la Fraise
STRAWBERRY-FILLED PASTRY FINGERS

★ ★ ★

MAKES ABOUT
12
ÉCLAIRS

PREPARATION TIME: 30 minutes (not including the cream puff dough)
COOKING TIME: 25 minutes · REFRIGERATION TIME: 4 hours

FOR THE STRAWBERRY CREAM: 5 large (3 ⅓ oz/95 g) egg yolks · ½ cup (3 ½ oz/100 g) granulated sugar · 3 tbsp plus 1 tsp (¾ oz/20 g) all-purpose flour · 1½ tbsp (½ oz/15 g) cornstarch · ¾ cup plus 1½ tbsp (200 mL) heavy whipping cream · 10 ¼ oz (290 g) store-bought strawberry purée · 1 (1/10 oz/3 g) gelatin sheet, or 1 tsp (1/10 oz/3 g) powdered gelatin · 2 tbsp (30 mL) very warm water · Strawberry extract (optional, used sparingly as the intensity of natural extracts varies · 1 stick plus 2 tbsp (5 ⅛ oz/145 g) unsalted butter, chilled and cut into pieces
FOR THE CREAM PUFF DOUGH: See the recipe on page 106
FOR THE STRAWBERRY GLAZE: 1¾ oz (50 g) premium couverture white chocolate, in disks or evenly chopped · 1 tbsp (15 mL) sweetened condensed milk · 1 tbsp (½ oz/14 g) unsalted butter · 1½ (⅛ oz/5 g) gelatin sheets, or 1½ tsp (⅛ oz/5 g) powdered gelatin · 2 tbsp (30 mL) very warm water · 2 tbsp plus 2 ½ tsp (1 ¼ oz/35 g) granulated sugar plus 2 tbsp (1 ¼ oz/35 g) glucose syrup (or corn syrup), or ¼ cup plus 1 tbsp plus 1¾ tsp (2 ½ oz/70 g) granulated sugar · 1 small pinch powdered red food color · 14 oz (400 g) fresh strawberries

＊ Make the strawberry cream. In a medium bowl, vigorously whisk together the egg yolks and sugar until lightened. Add the flour and cornstarch and whisk to combine. In a saucepan, warm the cream with the strawberry purée. Pour the cream mixture over the egg mixture while whisking constantly. Pour the entire mixture back into the saucepan and cook over medium heat, stirring constantly, until very thick, about 5 minutes.

Éclairs á la fraise ou pistache-framboises
STRAWBERRY-FILLED OR PISTACHIO PASTRY FINGERS

* Soak the gelatin sheet for 10 minutes in a bowl of cold water. (If using powdered gelatin, sprinkle it over 1 tbsp plus 2 tsp (25 mL) cold water and stir to moisten it; let soften for 5 minutes.) Squeeze the water from the gelatin sheet and add it to the warm water; stir to dissolve. Stir the gelatin mixture into the warm custard (or stir in the softened powdered gelatin, if using, until fully melted) and the strawberry extract, if using. Let cool slightly.

* Add the butter pieces to the cream. Using an immersion blender, blend the mixture until smooth and the butter is incorporated. Cover the surface with plastic wrap and refrigerate for at least 3 hours.

* Make the cream puff dough for éclairs following the step-by-step instructions on page 106.

* Bake for 25 minutes. Cool completely.

* Make the strawberry glaze. In a large mixing bowl, combine the chocolate, sweetened condensed milk, and butter. Soak the gelatin sheets for 10 minutes in a bowl of cold water. (If using powdered gelatin, sprinkle it over 2½ tbsp (40 mL) cold water and stir to moisten it; let soften for 5 minutes.) Squeeze the water from the gelatin sheets and add them to the warm water; stir to dissolve. In a small saucepan, heat the sugar and glucose syrup mixed with the food color and 1 tbsp (15 mL) water over high heat to 230°F/110°C; remove from the heat. Stir in the gelatin mixture (or stir in the softened powdered gelatin, if using, until fully melted), then pour the gelatin mixture into the bowl with the chocolate and whisk until smooth.

* Hold each éclair vertically over the bowl of glaze and generously coat one side of it using a small spatula. Hold the éclair over the bowl to allow any excess glaze to drip off, then run your finger around the border of the glazed area to wipe off any excess. Refrigerate for at least 1 hour to set the glaze.

* If necessary, briefly rinse the strawberries and pat them dry on paper towels. Hull the strawberries and slice them from top to bottom.

* To assemble the éclairs, split the éclairs lengthwise in half. Scrape the strawberry cream into a pastry bag fitted with a ⅓ -in (8-mm) plain pastry tube and fill the bottom half of the éclairs. Place strawberry slices on top of the strawberry cream. Replace the tops and refrigerate.

Variation: For Éclairs Pistache et Framboises/Pistachio and Raspberry Pastry Fingers, fill each half with a little store-bought raspberry sauce and pipe pistachio pastry cream on top (see the recipe on page 194). Place raspberries on top of the cream, replace the tops, and refrigerate.

Religieuses Passion

PASSION FRUIT CREAM PUFFS

★ ★ ★
MAKES ABOUT
8
RELIGIEUSES

PREPARATION TIME: 30 minutes (not including the dough) • COOKING TIME: 15 to 50 minutes • REFRIGERATION TIME: 4 hours

FOR THE PASSION FRUIT CREAM: 1¼ cups (9⅔ oz/275 g) store-bought passion fruit purée, or the juice and pulp from 12 to 14 fresh passion fruits (see Note, page 80) • 2 large (1⅓ oz/38 g) egg yolks • ¼ cup plus 1¼ tsp (2 oz/55 g) granulated sugar • 3 tbsp (1 oz/30 g) cornstarch • 1⅓ cups (300 mL) whole milk • 2 tbsp (1 oz/30 g) unsalted butter, chilled and cut into pieces

FOR THE CREAM PUFF DOUGH: See the recipe on page 106

FOR THE GLAZE: 1½ oz (40 g) premium couverture white chocolate, in disks or evenly chopped • ⅓ cup (80 mL) heavy whipping cream • ¼ cup plus 3 tbsp plus ½ tsp (3⅛ oz/90 g) granulated sugar • 1½ (⅛ oz/5 g) gelatin sheets, or 1½ tsp (⅛ oz/5 g) powdered gelatin • 2 tbsp (30 mL) very warm water • 1 small pinch powdered orange food color

* Make the passion fruit cream. If using fresh passion fruit, strain the juice and pulp over a bowl through a fine-mesh strainer to remove the seeds; measure out 1¼ cups (9⅔ oz/275 g) of the juice and pulp.

* In a medium bowl, vigorously whisk together the egg yolks and sugar just until lightened. Whisk in the cornstarch. In a saucepan, warm the milk with the passion fruit purée. Pour the milk mixture over the egg mixture while whisking constantly. Pour the entire mixture back into the saucepan and cook over medium heat, whisking constantly, until very thick, about 5 minutes. Let cool slightly. Add the butter pieces to the cream. Using an immersion blender, blend the mixture until smooth and the butter is incorporated. Cover the surface with plastic wrap and refrigerate for at least 3 hours.

* Make the cream puff dough following the step-by-step instructions on page 106. Line two baking sheets with parchment paper. Pipe eight puffs 2¼ in (6 cm) to 2¾ in (7 cm) in diameter on one sheet, and eight puffs 1⅛ in (3 cm) to 1½ in (4 cm) in diameter on the other. Place both baking sheets in the oven at the same time. Bake the smaller puffs for 15 minutes and the larger puffs for 25 minutes more. Cool completely.

* Use a ¼-in (6-mm) pastry tube to poke a hole in the bottom of each puff. Scrape the cream into a pastry bag fitted with a small plain pastry tube and fill the puffs.

* Make the glaze. Place the chocolate in a large bowl. In a small saucepan, combine the cream, sugar, and ¼ cup plus 1 tbsp (75 mL) water and bring it just to a boil. Pour the cream mixture over the chocolate. Let rest for several minutes, then whisk until smooth.

* Soak the gelatin sheets for 10 minutes in a bowl of cold water. (If using powdered gelatin, sprinkle it over 2½ tbsp (40 mL) cold water and stir to moisten; let soften for 5 minutes.) Squeeze the water from the gelatin sheets and add them to the warm water; stir to dissolve. Stir in the gelatin mixture (or the softened powdered gelatin, if using, until fully melted) and food color. Blend with an immersion blender until smooth. Cool completely.

* Hold each large puff over the bowl of glaze and coat one side of it using a small spatula. Hold the puffs over the bowl to allow any excess glaze to drip off while slowly turning them, then run your finger around the border of the glazed area to wipe off any excess. Place the glazed puffs on a plate. Next, glaze the smaller puffs and stick them to the tops of the larger ones. Refrigerate for at least 1 hour to allow the glaze to set.

Éclairs au Café

COFFEE-FILLED PASTRY FINGERS

★★★

MAKES ABOUT
12
ÉCLAIRS

PREPARATION TIME: 30 minutes (not including the dough) · COOKING TIME: 25 minutes · REFRIGERATION TIME: 4 hours

FOR THE COFFEE CREAM: 3 large (2 oz/57 g) egg yolks · ¼ cup plus 1 tbsp plus ½ tsp (2⅓ oz/65 g) granulated sugar · 1 tbsp (⅓ oz/10 g) cornstarch · 1 cup plus 2¾ tsp (250 mL) whole milk · ⅔ cup (150 mL) heavy whipping cream · 1 (1/10 oz/3 g) gelatin sheet, or 1 tsp (1/10 oz/3 g) powdered gelatin · 1 tbsp (15 mL) very warm water · 1 tbsp plus ½ tsp (¾ oz/20 g) coffee paste (see Note) · 1 stick minus ¾ tsp (3¾ oz/110 g) unsalted butter, room temperature

FOR THE CREAM PUFF DOUGH: See the recipe on page 106

FOR THE COFFEE GLAZE: 1¾ oz (50 g) premium couverture white chocolate, in disks or evenly chopped · 1 tsp (5 mL) coffee extract (see Note) · 1 tbsp (15 mL) sweetened condensed milk · 1 tbsp (½ oz/14 g) unsalted butter · 1½ (⅛ oz/5 g) gelatin sheets, or 1½ tsp (⅛ oz/5 g) powdered gelatin · 2 tbsp (30 mL) very warm water · 2 tbsp plus 2½ tsp (1¼ oz/35 g) granulated sugar plus 2 tbsp (1¼ oz/35 g) glucose syrup (or corn syrup), or ¼ cup plus 1 tbsp plus 1¾ tsp (2½ oz/70 g) granulated sugar

* Make the coffee cream. In a medium bowl, vigorously whisk together the egg yolks and sugar until lightened. Whisk in the cornstarch. In a saucepan, warm the milk with the cream. Pour the milk mixture over the egg mixture while whisking constantly. Pour the entire mixture back into the saucepan and cook over medium heat, whisking constantly, until very thick, about 5 minutes.

* Soak the gelatin sheet for 10 minutes in a bowl of cold water. (If using powdered gelatin, sprinkle it over 1 tbsp plus 2 tsp (25 mL) cold water and stir to moisten it; let soften for 5 minutes.) Squeeze the water from the gelatin sheet and add it to the warm water; stir to dissolve. Stir the gelatin mixture (or stir in the softened powdered gelatin, if using, until fully melted) and coffee paste into the warm custard. Let cool slightly. Add the butter pieces to the custard. Using an immersion blender, blend the mixture until smooth and the butter is incorporated. Cover the surface with plastic wrap and refrigerate for at least 3 hours.

* Make the cream puff dough for éclairs following the step-by-step instructions on page 106. Bake for 25 minutes. Cool completely.

* Use a ¼-in (6-mm) pastry tube to poke two holes in the bottom of each shell through which to pipe the filling. Scrape the cream into a pastry bag fitted with a plain pastry tube and fill the éclairs.

* Make the coffee glaze. In a large mixing bowl, combine the chocolate, coffee extract, sweetened condensed milk, and butter. Soak the gelatin sheets for 10 minutes in a bowl of cold water. (If using powdered gelatin, sprinkle it over 2½ tbsp (40 mL) cold water and stir to moisten it; let soften for 5 minutes.) Squeeze the water from the gelatin sheets and add them to the warm water; stir to dissolve.

* In a small saucepan, heat the sugar, glucose syrup, and 1 tbsp (15 mL) water over high heat to 230°F/110°C; remove from the heat. Stir in the gelatin mixture (or stir in the softened powdered gelatin, if using, until fully melted), then pour the gelatin mixture into the bowl with the chocolate and whisk until smooth.

* Hold each filled éclair vertically over the bowl of glaze and coat one side of it using a small spatula.

* Hold the éclair over the bowl to allow any excess glaze to drip off, then run your finger around the border of the glazed area to wipe off any excess. Refrigerate for at least 1 hour to allow the glaze to set.

Éclairs au Chocolat

CHOCOLATE-FILLED PASTRY FINGERS

★ ★ ★

MAKES ABOUT
12
ÉCLAIRS

PREPARATION TIME: 30 minutes (not including the dough) · COOKING TIME: 25 minutes · REFRIGERATION TIME: 4 hours

FOR THE CHOCOLATE CREAM: 3 large (2 oz/57 g) egg yolks · ¼ cup plus 1 tbsp plus ½ tsp (2 ⅓ oz/65 g) granulated sugar · 1 tbsp (⅓ oz/10 g) cornstarch · 1 cup plus 2 ¾ tsp (250 mL) whole milk · ⅔ cup (150 mL) heavy whipping cream · 5 ½ oz (160 g) premium couverture dark chocolate, in disks or evenly chopped

FOR THE CREAM PUFF DOUGH: See the recipe on page 106

FOR THE CHOCOLATE GLAZE: 1¾ oz (50 g) premium couverture dark chocolate, in disks or evenly chopped · 1 tbsp (15 mL) sweetened condensed milk · 1 tbsp (½ oz/14 g) unsalted butter · 1½ (⅛ oz/5 g) gelatin sheets, or 1½ tsp (⅛ oz/5 g) powdered gelatin · 2 tbsp (30 mL) very warm water · 2 tbsp plus 2 ½ tsp (1¼ oz/35 g) granulated sugar plus 2 tbsp (1¼ oz/35 g) glucose syrup (or corn syrup), or ¼ cup plus 1 tbsp plus 1¾ tsp (2 ½ oz/70 g) granulated sugar

＊ **Make the chocolate cream.** In a medium bowl, vigorously whisk together the egg yolks and sugar until lightened. Whisk in the cornstarch. In a saucepan, warm the milk with the cream, then pour the milk mixture over the egg mixture while whisking constantly. Pour the entire mixture back into the saucepan and cook over medium heat, whisking constantly, until very thick, about 5 minutes. Whisk in the chocolate until fully melted. Let cool slightly. Blend until smooth using an immersion blender. Cover the surface with plastic wrap and refrigerate for at least 3 hours.

＊ **Make the cream puff dough** for éclairs following the step-by-step instructions on page 106. Bake for 25 minutes. Cool completely. Use a ¼-in (6-mm) pastry tube to poke two holes in the bottom of each shell through which to pipe the filling. Scrape the cream into a pastry bag fitted with a plain pastry tube and fill the éclairs.

＊ **Make the chocolate glaze.** In a large mixing bowl, combine the chocolate, sweetened condensed milk, and butter. Soak the gelatin sheets for 10 minutes in a bowl of cold water. (If using powdered gelatin, sprinkle it over 2 ½ tbsp (40 mL) cold water and stir to moisten it; let soften for 5 minutes.) Squeeze the water from the gelatin sheets and add them to the warm water; stir to dissolve.

＊ In a small saucepan, heat the sugar, glucose syrup, and 1 tbsp (15 mL) water over high heat to 230°F/110°C; remove from the heat. Stir in the gelatin mixture (or stir in the softened powdered gelatin, if using, until fully melted), then pour the gelatin mixture into the bowl with the chocolate and whisk until smooth.

＊ Hold each filled éclair vertically over the bowl of glaze and coat one side of it using a small spatula.

＊ Hold the éclair over the bowl to allow any excess glaze to drip off, then run your finger around the border of the glazed area to wipe off any excess. Refrigerate for at least 1 hour to allow the glaze to set.

Saint-Honoré

LAYERED PUFF PASTRY CAKE WITH
CHANTILLY CREAM AND CARAMEL GLAZE

★ ★ ★

SERVES
6 to 8

PREPARATION TIME: 35 minutes (not including the cream puff dough) · COOKING TIME: 15 to 35 minutes

10 ½ oz (300 g) all-butter puff pastry dough, homemade (see page 134) or store-bought, fresh or frozen

FOR THE PASTRY CREAM: ¼ cup plus 2 tbsp (2½ oz/75 g) granulated sugar · 2 large (1⅓ oz/38 g) egg yolks · 3 tbsp (1 oz/30 g) cornstarch · 1⅓ cups (300 mL) whole milk · 1 vanilla bean · 3 tbsp plus ½ tsp (1½ oz/45 g) unsalted butter, chilled and cut into pieces

FOR THE CREAM PUFF DOUGH: See the recipe on page 106

FOR THE CARAMEL: ¾ cup (5¼ oz/150 g) granulated sugar

FOR THE CHANTILLY CREAM: ½ vanilla bean · ¾ cup plus 1½ tbsp (200 mL) heavy whipping cream, well chilled · ¼ cup minus 2 tsp (¾ oz/20 g) confectioners' sugar, sifted

* Make the pastry cream following the step-by-step instructions on page 138.

* Make the cream puff dough for Saint-Honoré following the step-by-step instructions on page 106.

* Preheat the oven to 350°F/180°C. Line two baking sheets with parchment paper. Roll out the puff pastry dough to a thickness of ⅛ in (3 mm). Cut out a circle 8½ in (22 cm) in diameter and transfer it to one of the baking sheets. Pipe the cream puff dough around the edge of the puff pastry dough circle (following the step-by-step instructions on pages 106, 108).

* On the second baking sheet, pipe puffs 1⅛ in (3 cm) to 1½ in (4 cm) in diameter using the remaining cream puff dough (about 20 puffs). Place both baking sheets in the oven. Bake the puffs for 15 minutes, and the ring for 35 minutes (1).

* Use a ¼-in (6-mm) plain pastry tube to poke a hole in the bottom of each puff (2).

* Scrape the pastry cream into a pastry bag fitted with a plain pastry tube and fill the puffs (3).

* Make the caramel. In a heavy saucepan, combine the sugar with 3 tbsp plus 1 tsp (50 mL) water (4) and cook over high heat, stirring frequently.

* When the caramel has turned a pale amber color, remove the saucepan from the heat and dip it into a bowl of cold water to stop the cooking (5).

* Dip the tops of the filled puffs into the caramel and place them on a piece of parchment paper with the caramel sides down (6).

* Let the puffs cool, then dip the bottoms of the puffs in a little bit of the caramel and stick them around the edge of the bottom disk (7) to (9).

* Make the chantilly cream. Cut the vanilla bean in half lengthwise and scrape the seeds out into the cream using a small paring knife. Beat the cream with the confectioners' sugar into medium-stiff peaks. (10)

* Scrape the whipped cream into a pastry bag fitted with a Saint-Honoré tube (or a large plain pastry tube) and pipe the cream into the center of the cake in a chevron pattern (11).

* If there are leftover puffs, place them on top of the cream in the center of the cake.

* Refrigerate until ready to serve.

Saint-Honoré

LAYERED PUFF PASTRY CAKE WITH CHANTILLY CREAM AND CARAMEL GLAZE

Les Incontournables

CLASSIC AND TIMELESS CAKES

Pâte Feuilletée

PUFF PASTRY DOUGH (IN THREE TURNS)

★ ★ ★

**MAKES ABOUT
2½ LB (1.2 KG) PUFF
PASTRY DOUGH**

PREPARATION TIME: 30 minutes

REFRIGERATION TIME: 2 hours (3 times)—6 hours total

5 ⅓ cups (1 ⅛ lb/530 g) all-purpose flour • 2 tsp (½ oz/12 g) salt • 3 tbsp plus 1 ¾ tsp (1 ¾ oz/50 g) unsalted butter, room temperature plus 3 sticks plus 2 tbsp, plus 2 tsp (13 ½ oz/380 g) unsalted butter, well chilled

* Puff pastry ingredients (1).
* In the bowl of a standing mixer fitted with the dough hook, place the flour, salt, softened butter, and ¾ cup plus 1½ tbsp (200 mL) water (2) to (5).
* Knead the mixture on low just until it forms a smooth mass (you can also do this by hand) (6).
* Turn the dough out onto a work surface and form it into a ball (7). Refrigerate for 2 hours. (This first base dough mixture is called the *détrampe*.)
* Remove the chilled butter from the refrigerator, place it between two sheets of parchment paper, and roll it out to about an 8 ½-in (22-cm) square (8) (9).
* Flour a work surface and roll out the détrampe to a 10-in (25-cm) by 20-in (50-cm) rectangle (10).
* Place the butter square on top of the dough rectangle flush with the top end (11) and fold the bottom half of the dough over it (12).
* Press the edges of the dough together to seal (13).
* Turn the dough one quarter turn to the right and roll it out so that its length is three times its width (14).

* Fold the bottom half of the dough in toward the middle with its edge positioned at the center (15).
* Fold the top half of the dough in toward the middle with its edge against the edge of the bottom half (16).
* Fold the dough in half over onto itself (as if closing a book) (17).
* Wrap the dough in plastic wrap.
* Press your fingertip into the dough to mark it as the first turn (18).
* Refrigerate for 2 hours.
* Repeat steps 14 through 17. Press two fingertips into the dough to mark it as the second turn. Refrigerate for 2 hours.
* Repeat steps 14 through 17 (the third turn). Cut the dough in half and roll it out according to the instructions in the recipe, or place it back in the refrigerator to keep for 4 to 5 days.

Note: You can divide the dough into three or four portions weighing between 10 ½ oz (300 g) and 14 oz (400 g) each (according to your needs), wrap tightly, and freeze in large freezer bags. Let thaw for 24 hours in the refrigerator before using.

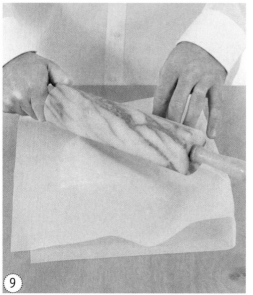

Pâte Feuilletée

PUFF PASTRY DOUGH (IN THREE TURNS)

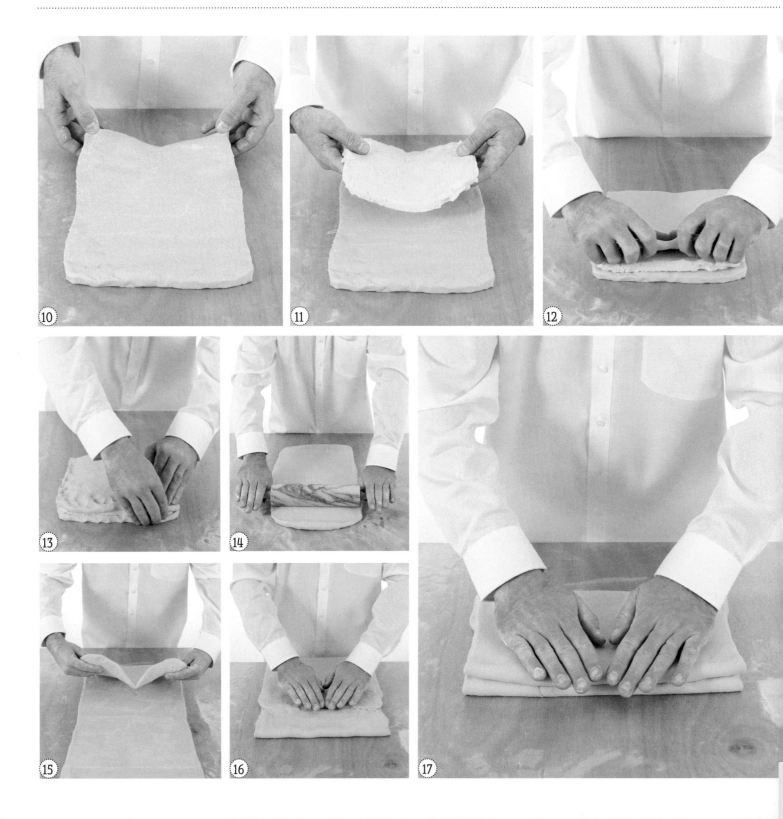

Crème Pâtissière

PASTRY CREAM

★ ★ ★

**MAKES
4 ¼ CUPS (1 L)
PASTRY CREAM**

PREPARATION TIME: 5 minutes • COOKING TIME: 5 minutes • REFRIGERATION TIME: 3 hours

4 large (2 ⅔ oz/76 g) egg yolks • ¾ cup (5 ¼ oz/150 g) granulated sugar • ¼ cup plus 2 tbsp (2 ⅛ oz/60 g) cornstarch • 2 ½ cups (600 mL) whole milk

Pastry Cream Ingredients ①

* In a medium bowl, vigorously whisk together the egg yolks and sugar until lightened ② to ④.
* Whisk in the cornstarch ⑤ to ⑥.
* In a saucepan, warm the milk, then slowly pour it into the egg mixture while whisking constantly ⑦ to ⑧.
* Pour the entire mixture back into the saucepan and cook over medium heat, whisking constantly, until very thick, about 5 minutes ⑨ to ⑪.
* Scrape the pastry cream into a large bowl. Cover the surface with plastic wrap and refrigerate ⑫ for 3 hours.

Variations (according to the recipes on pages 120 and 128):

Pastry Cream with Gelatin

* Soak the gelatin sheets (according to the quantity in the recipe) for 10 minutes in a bowl of cold water. (If using powdered gelatin, sprinkle it over cold water according to the quantities in each recipe and stir to moisten it; let soften for 5 minutes.) Squeeze the water from the gelatin sheets and add them to the warm water or mixture, according to the recipe (for the recipe above, use 2 tbsp/30 mL warm water); stir to dissolve. Stir the gelatin mixture into the pastry cream (or stir in the softened powdered gelatin, if using) until fully melted.

Pastry Cream with Butter

* Add cold, unsalted butter (use ¾ stick plus 1 tsp (3 ⅛ oz/90 g) for the recipe above) that has been cut into pieces and blend it, one piece at a time, into the cream using an immersion blender. Cover the surface with plastic wrap and refrigerate.

Note: The flavors added will vary according to the recipe. The classic flavoring is vanilla, typically in powdered form. You can also cut a vanilla bean in half lengthwise and scrape out the seeds and add them and the empty pod to the hot milk (discarding the pod at the end).

Crème Pâtissière

PASTRY CREAM

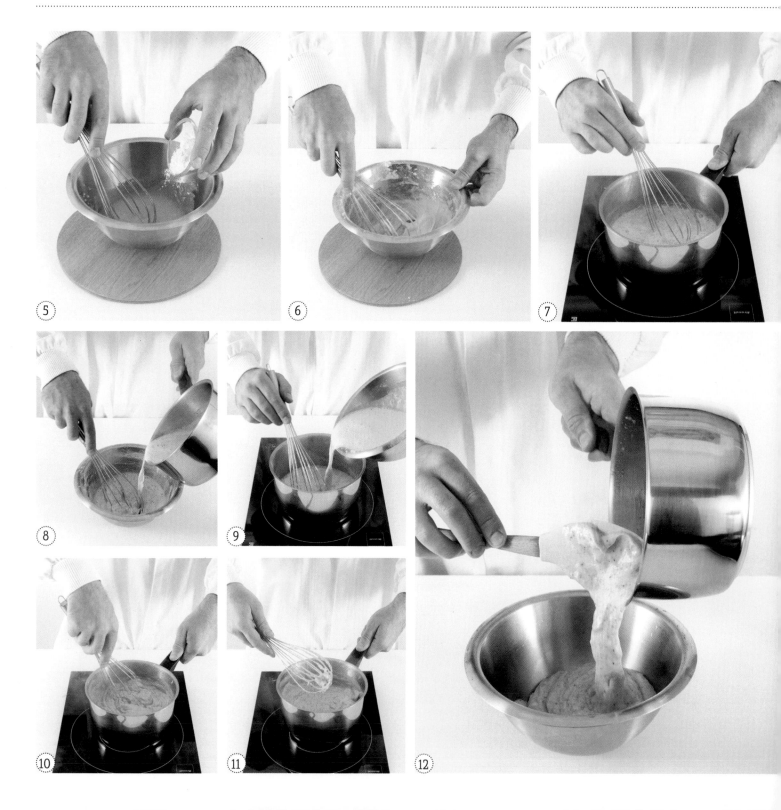

LAYERED CREAM-FILLED PASTRY

★ ★ ★

SERVES
6 to 8
(SEE NOTE)

PREPARATION TIME: 25 minutes (not including the puff pastry dough) ·
REFRIGERATION TIME: 2 hours · COOKING TIME: 35 minutes

FOR THE CREAM FILLING: 2 large (1⅓ oz/38 g) egg yolks · ¼ cup plus 2 tbsp (2½ oz/75 g) granulated sugar · 3 tbsp (1 oz/30 g) cornstarch · 1⅓ cups (300 mL) whole milk · 1 vanilla bean, split and seeds scraped out, pod reserved · 4 (½ oz/12 g) gelatin sheets, or 1 tbsp plus 1 tsp (½ oz/12 g) powdered gelatin · 2 tbsp (30 mL) very warm water · 3 tbsp plus ½ tsp (1½ oz/45 g) unsalted butter, chilled and cut into pieces · ⅔ cup (150 mL) heavy whipping cream, well chilled
FOR THE PUFF PASTRY DOUGH: 14 oz (400 g) all-butter puff pastry dough, homemade (see page 134) or store-bought, fresh or frozen · ½ cup (1¾ oz/50 g) confectioners' sugar
FOR THE DECORATION: ¼ cup (1 oz/25 g) confectioners' sugar

* Make the cream filling. This cream is made in the same way as pastry cream, following the step-by-step instructions on page 138.

* In a medium bowl, vigorously whisk together the egg yolks and sugar until lightened. Whisk in the cornstarch. In a saucepan, warm the milk and the vanilla seeds and pod. Slowly pour the milk mixture into the egg mixture while whisking constantly. Pour the entire mixture back into the saucepan and cook over medium heat, whisking constantly, until very thick, about 5 minutes. Discard the pod.

* Soak the gelatin sheets for 10 minutes in a bowl of cold water. (If using powdered gelatin, sprinkle it over ¼ cup plus 2½ tbsp (100 mL) cold water and stir to moisten it; let soften for 5 minutes.) Squeeze the water from the gelatin sheets and add them to the warm water; stir to dissolve. Stir the gelatin into the warm custard (or stir in the softened powdered gelatin, if using, until fully melted). Let cool slightly. Add the butter pieces to the custard. Using an immersion blender, blend the mixture until smooth and the butter is incorporated. Cover the surface with plastic wrap and refrigerate until cooled.

Mille-Feuille

LAYERED CREAM-FILLED PASTRY

* Whip the cream, then fold it into the cooled custard mixture using a silicone spatula or whisk (1) to (3). Cover the surface with plastic wrap and refrigerate for at least 2 hours.

* Bake the puff pastry. Preheat the oven to 350°F/180°C. Line a baking sheet with parchment paper. Roll out the puff pastry dough ⅛ in (3 mm) thick into a rectangle that will fit on your baking sheet. Transfer the dough to the baking sheet, then place a piece of parchment paper on top to cover it. Place a second baking sheet on top to prevent puffing during baking. Bake for 30 minutes. Cool completely.

* Depending on the size of your serving plate, carefully cut the pastry into three squares, rectangles, or circles of equal size (you can cut out a cardboard template as a guide).

* Sift a layer of confectioners' sugar on top of one of the layers (4) and bake it for 5 minutes at 450°F/240°C, watching it carefully so that it caramelizes but does not burn.

* Assemble the mille-feuille (5). Scrape the cream into a pastry bag fitted with an open star pastry tube (6).

* Pipe a layer of cream rosettes on top of one of the non-caramelized layers (7) to (8).

* Cover the rosettes with one of the puff pastry layers (9) and pipe a second layer of cream rosettes (10).

* Place the caramelized puff pastry layer on top (11).

* Place parallel strips of paper on top at a diagonal and dust with confectioners' sugar.

* Carefully lift off the strips to reveal the striped pattern (12).

* Pipe one or two rosettes on top for decoration (optional).

Note: For individual mille-feuilles, cut out three 1½ in (4 cm) by 3-in (8-cm) rectangles per person.

4

5

6

7

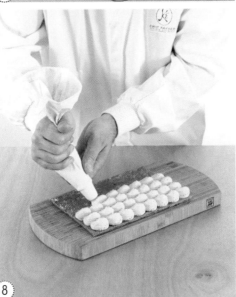

8

9

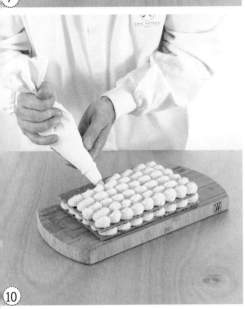

10

11

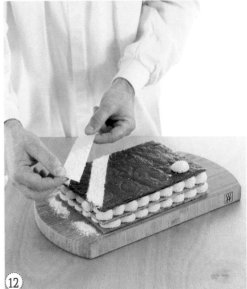

12

Mille-Feuille aux Fruits Rouges

LAYERED CREAM-FILLED PASTRY WITH BERRIES

★ ★ ★

SERVES
6 to 8

PREPARATION TIME: 25 minutes (not including the puff pastry dough) · COOKING TIME: 40 minutes

Assemble 1⅛ lb (500 g) of fresh, halved strawberries (or raspberries, blackberries, or a mixture thereof) into 2 equal portions, leaving a few berries for garnish, plus one recipe of pastry cream (page 144), and three puff pastry rounds (page 142). (1). Place one portion on top of the cream in the lower two layers (2) to (8), and top with the third pastry layer.

Succés

CHOCOLATE-PRALINE MERINGUE CAKE

★ ★ ★

SERVES
6 to 8

PREPARATION TIME: 60 minutes · REFRIGERATION TIME: 2 hours, plus overnight
COOKING TIME: 12 minutes · FREEZING TIME: 30 minutes
One 6-in (16-cm) square cake ring

FOR THE PRALINE GANACHE: 1 (1/10 oz/3 g) gelatin sheet, or 1 tsp (1/10 oz/3 g) powdered gelatin · ¾ cup plus 1½ tbsp (200 mL) heavy whipping cream · 1 tbsp (15 mL) very warm water · 1¾ oz (50 g) premium couverture white chocolate, in disks or evenly chopped · 2⅛ oz (60 g) praline paste
FOR THE DACQUOISE (NUT MERINGUE): 5 large (6⅓ oz/180 g) egg whites · ½ cup (3½ oz/100 g) granulated sugar · ½ cup plus 2 tsp (2 oz/55 g) confectioners' sugar, sifted · ¼ cup plus 1 tbsp (1 oz/30 g) all-purpose flour · 1¼ cups (3½ oz/100 g) hazelnut flour · ¾ cup (3½ oz/100 g) hazelnuts, coarsely chopped
FOR THE DARK CHOCOLATE GANACHE: 4 oz (115 g) premium couverture dark chocolate, in disks or evenly chopped · ½ cup (120 mL) heavy whipping cream · 3 tbsp plus ½ tsp (1½ oz/40 g) granulated sugar · 1 tbsp plus 1 tsp (¾ oz/20 g) unsalted butter

* Make the praline ganache. Soak the gelatin sheet for 10 minutes in a bowl of cold water. (If using powdered gelatin, sprinkle it over 1 tbsp plus 2 tsp (25 mL) cold water and stir to moisten it; let soften for 5 minutes.)

* In a small saucepan, bring the cream to a boil ⋅1⋅.

* Squeeze the water from the gelatin sheet and add it to the warm water; stir to dissolve. Stir the gelatin mixture into the warm cream (or stir in the softened powdered gelatin, if using, until fully melted). Place the chocolate and the praline paste in a bowl ⋅2⋅ and pour the warm cream mixture over it. ⋅3⋅

Succés

CHOCOLATE-PRALINE MERINGUE CAKE

* Using an immersion blender, blend the mixture until smooth. Cover the surface with plastic wrap and refrigerate for at least 2 hours.

* Make the dacquoise. Preheat the oven to 350°F/180°C. Line a rimmed baking sheet with parchment paper. In the bowl of a standing mixer fitted with the whisk attachment, beat the egg whites into stiff peaks, adding the sugar a little at a time halfway through the beating time (4).

* In a large bowl, combine the confectioners' sugar, all-purpose flour, and hazelnut flour (5) to (6).

* Fold the beaten egg whites into the flour-nut mixture (7) to (8).

* Spread the nut meringue into a thin layer on the prepared baking sheet (three 6-in [15-cm] squares of dacquoise are needed, one with hazelnuts) (9).

* Sprinkle one-third of the meringue with the chopped hazelnuts (10) and bake for 12 minutes.

* Cool completely. Carefully peel the parchment paper off the bottom of the dacquoise.

* Make the dark chocolate ganache. Place the chocolate in a large bowl. In a saucepan, bring the cream and sugar to a boil and pour it over the chocolate (11).

* Stir until thoroughly combined (12).

* Add the butter pieces to the cream. Using an immersion blender, blend the mixture until smooth and the butter is incorporated (13) to (14).

* Assemble the Succès. In the bowl of a standing mixer fitted with the whisk attachment, beat the praline ganache just until lightened (15). Scrape it into a pastry bag fitted with a large plain pastry tube.

* Using the cake ring, cut out a piece of the dacquoise with chopped hazelnuts to serve as the top layer (16). Using the ring, cut two more layers out of the plain dacquoise (17) (if needed, you can assemble smaller pieces of the dacquoise to create the center layer).

* Place the cake ring onto a serving plate. Place a plain layer inside on the bottom and pour in half of the chocolate ganache (18). Freeze for 15 minutes.

* Scrape the praline ganache into a piping bag fitted with a plain pastry tube. Pipe half of the praline ganache on top of the frozen ganache layer (19).

* Add a second plain dacquoise layer on top and pour the remaining chocolate ganache over the top (20). Freeze for 15 minutes.

* Pipe the remaining praline ganache on top and spread it out evenly (21).

* Place the dacquoise layer with the chopped nuts on top (22).

* Refrigerate overnight. Just before serving, carefully remove the ring (23) to (24).

4

5

6

7

8

9

0

11

12

Succés

CHOCOLATE-PRALINE MERINGUE CAKE

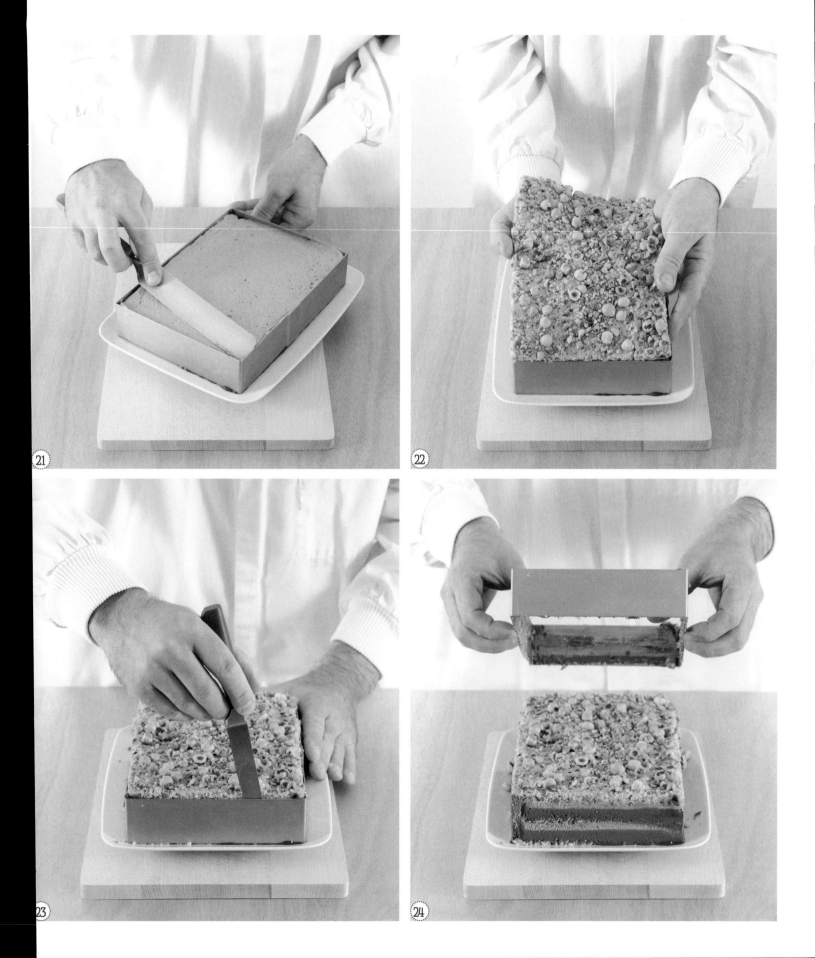

Opéra

LAYERED COFFEE-ALMOND CREAM CAKE

★ ★ ★

SERVES
6 to 8

PREPARATION TIME: 1 hour · REFRIGERATION TIME: 2 hours, plus overnight · COOKING TIME: 20 minutes

One 7-in (18-cm) or 8-in (20-cm) round or square cake ring

FOR THE COFFEE SYRUP: ½ cup (3½ oz/100 g) granulated sugar · ½ tsp (3 mL) coffee extract · 1 tsp (1/10 oz/2 g) instant coffee

FOR THE LADYFINGERS SPONGE CAKE: ½ cup minus 2½ tsp (1½ oz/45 g) all-purpose flour · 3 large (3⅛ oz/90 g) egg whites · ½ cup (3½ oz/100 g) granulated sugar · 5 large (3⅓ oz/95 g) egg yolks

FOR THE ITALIAN MERINGUE: ¼ cup plus 2½ tsp (2⅛ oz/60 g) granulated sugar · 1 large (1 oz/30 g) egg white

FOR THE COFFEE BUTTERCREAM: 3 tbsp plus 1 tsp (50 mL) whole milk · 1 tsp (1/10 oz/2 g) coarsely crushed coffee beans · 1 large (⅔ oz/19 g) egg yolk · 1 tbsp plus 1¾ tsp (¾ oz/20 g) granulated sugar · 1 tsp (1/10 oz/2 g) instant coffee · 1 stick plus 3 tbsp plus 1 tsp (5½ oz/160 g) unsalted butter, room temperature

FOR THE DARK CHOCOLATE GANACHE: 7½ oz (215 g) premium couverture 62% cacao dark chocolate, in disks or evenly chopped · 1 cup plus 2¾ tsp (250 mL) light whipping cream · ¼ cup (1¾ oz/50 g) granulated sugar · ¾ stick plus 2 tsp (3⅓ oz/95 g) unsalted butter

FOR THE GLAZE (SEE NOTE): 2½ oz (75 g) premium couverture 62% cacao dark chocolate, in disks or evenly chopped · 1 tbsp plus 2 tsp (1 oz/25 g) unsalted butter

FOR THE DECORATION: Chocolate-covered coffee beans and edible gold leaf

* Make the coffee syrup. In a saucepan, combine the sugar, coffee extract, instant coffee, and ¼ cup plus 2½ tbsp (100 mL) water. Bring to a boil. Remove from the heat and set aside, covered.

* Make the ladyfingers sponge cake. Preheat the oven to 350°F/180°C. Line a rimmed sheet pan with parchment paper.

* Follow the step-by-step instructions for the Charlotte ladyfingers recipe on page 168 (but do not pipe into fingers). Sift the flour. In the bowl of a standing mixer fitted with the whisk attachment, beat the egg whites into stiff peaks, adding the sugar a little at a time halfway through the beating time. Reduce the speed to low, and add the egg yolks. Beat until incorporated and transfer the mixture to a bowl. Carefully fold in the flour, just until incorporated. Spread the batter evenly into the prepared sheet pan (you will need three 7- or 8-in [18- or 20-cm] layers to assemble the cake). Bake for 10 minutes.

* Make the Italian meringue. In a small heavy saucepan, heat the sugar and 1 tbsp (15 mL) water over high heat to 250°F/121°C. (If you do not have a candy thermometer, drop a small quantity of the hot syrup into a bowl of cold water. It should form a ball and feel soft when pinched between your fingers) 1 .

* Meanwhile, using a handheld mixer, begin beating the egg white on medium speed until soft peaks form. When the syrup reaches 250°F/121°C, pour it in a steady stream down the inside edge of the bowl and continue beating until all of the syrup is incorporated and the egg white is stiff and glossy 2 to 3 .

* Cake ingredients 4

* Make the coffee buttercream. In a small saucepan, bring the milk to a boil and add the crushed coffee beans to infuse 5 .

* Let cool, then strain through a fine-mesh strainer 6 .

Opéra

LAYERED COFFEE-ALMOND CREAM CAKE

* In a large bowl, whisk the egg yolk and sugar. Reheat the infused milk, add the instant coffee, then whisk it into the egg mixture (7).

* Pour the combined mixture back into the saucepan and cook it over very low heat, stirring constantly, until the mixture coats the back of the spoon, about 5 minutes (8). Cool completely.

* In the bowl of a standing mixer fitted with the whisk attachment, beat the butter until creamy. Beat in the cooked cream a little at a time until incorporated (9), then fold this mixture into the Italian meringue (10).

* Make the dark chocolate ganache following the step-by-step photos for the Succès chocolate ganache on page 150. Place the chocolate in a large bowl. In a saucepan, bring the cream and sugar to a boil and pour it over the chocolate. Stir until thoroughly combined.

* Add the butter pieces to the chocolate mixture. Using an immersion blender, blend the mixture until smooth and the butter is incorporated.

* Assemble the Opéra. Cut the sponge into three equal circles or squares using the cake ring (if necessary, you can assemble smaller pieces of the cake for the center layer) (11).

* Place the ring on a serving plate and place one of the cake layers on the bottom. Using a pastry brush, brush the cake layer with coffee syrup (12).

* Evenly spread half of the chocolate ganache on top of the cake layer, then add a second cake layer on top and brush it with coffee syrup (13) to (14).

* Evenly spread the buttercream on top and smooth it out (15).

* Place the last layer of cake on top and brush it with coffee syrup (16) to (17).

* Evenly spread the remaining ganache on top (leaving enough room at the top to accommodate the glaze).

* Refrigerate for at least 2 hours.

* Make the glaze. In a heatproof bowl set over a pot of simmering water, gently melt the chocolate with the butter (or place them in a microwave-safe bowl and microwave for 1 minute), then stir until completely melted. Let cool slightly, then carefully pour it on top of the cake (18).

* For special occasions, you can decorate the cake with a piece of edible gold leaf in addition to the coffee beans. Delicately pick up the gold leaf with the point of a knife and place it in random spots on top of the cake (19). Be careful, as the smallest breeze can carry the gold leaf away as easily as a feather (20)!

* Refrigerate overnight. Remove the ring just before serving.

Note: To make a glaze with a professional appearance, follow the chocolate glaze recipe on page 164.

Opéra

LAYERED COFFEE-ALMOND CREAM CAKE

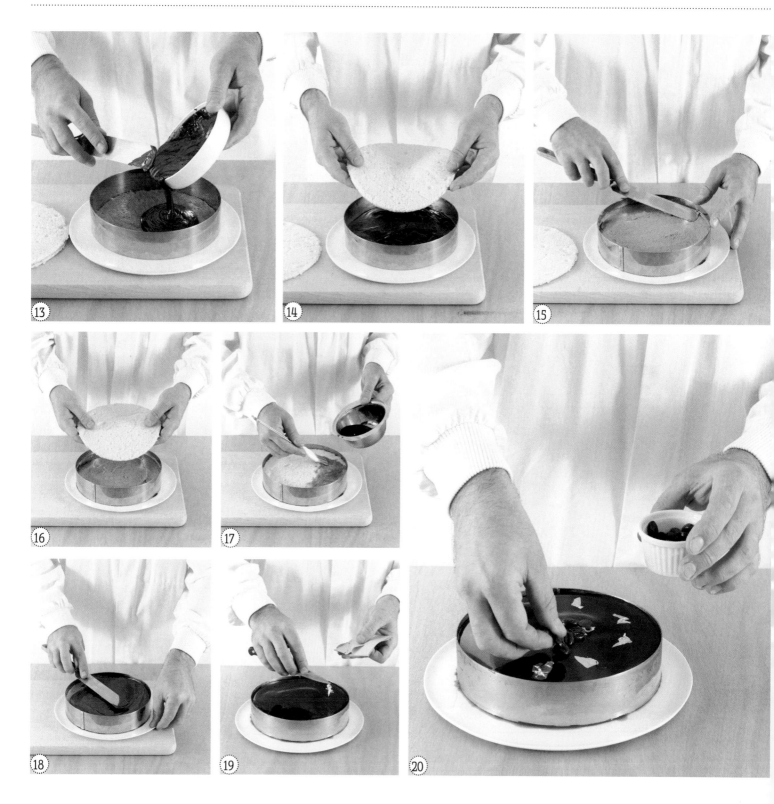

Fraisier

STRAWBERRY CREAM CAKE

★ ★ ★

SERVES
6 to 8

PREPARATION TIME: 1 hour · COOKING TIME: 15 minutes · REFRIGERATION TIME: Overnight
One 8-in (20-cm) round cake ring

FOR THE PASTRY CREAM: 3 large (2 oz/57 g) egg yolks · ½ cup plus 1 tbsp plus ½ tsp (4 oz/115 g) granulated sugar · ¼ cup plus ¾ tbsp (1½ oz/45 g) cornstarch · 1¾ cups plus 2 tbsp (450 mL) whole milk · 1 stick plus 3 tbsp (5¼ oz/150 g) unsalted butter, room temperature
FOR THE SPONGE CAKE: ½ cup plus 2½ tbsp (2⅓ oz/65 g) all-purpose flour · 7 large (4⅔ oz/133 g) egg yolks · ¾ cup plus 2 tbsp plus 1¼ tsp (6⅓ oz/180 g) granulated sugar, divided · 4 large (4¼ oz/120 g) egg whites
FOR THE FILLING AND TOPPING: 1⅛ lb (500 g) fresh whole strawberries

* Make the pastry cream following the step-by-step instructions on page 138. In a medium bowl, vigorously whisk together the egg yolks and sugar until lightened. Whisk in the cornstarch. In a saucepan, warm the milk, then slowly pour it into the egg mixture while whisking constantly. Pour the combined mixture back into the saucepan and cook over medium heat, whisking constantly, until very thick, about 5 minutes. Cover the surface with plastic wrap and refrigerate.

* Preheat the oven to 350°F/180°C. Line a rimmed sheet pan with parchment paper.

* Make the sponge cake. Sift the flour. In a large bowl, whisk together the egg yolks and one-third of the sugar until lightened. In a separate bowl,

beat the egg whites into stiff peaks, adding the remaining sugar a little at a time halfway through the beating time. Fold the beaten egg whites into the yolk mixture, then fold in the flour. Spread the batter evenly into the prepared sheet pan. Bake for 10 minutes. Cool completely.

* Carefully peel the parchment paper from the cake.

* Assemble the Fraisier. Using the cake ring, cut out two circles from the cake.

* Add the butter to the bowl of a standing mixer fitted with the whisk attachment and beat until light and creamy ①to ②.

* Add the pastry cream and beat until well incorporated. Transfer the mixture to a bowl ③ to ④.

Fraisier

STRAWBERRY CREAM CAKE

* Place the cake ring on a serving plate and place one cake circle on the bottom (5).

* If necessary, briefly rinse the strawberries and pat them dry on paper towels.

* Set aside one dozen of the most attractive strawberries for the top decoration. Hull and cut similarly sized strawberries in half and place them next to each other around the perimeter of the ring with the cut side touching the ring (6).

* Cover the strawberries with a little of the pastry cream to seal them against the ring (7).

* Hull the remaining ones and place in the center of the cake (8).

* Cover the layer of strawberries with some of the pastry cream (9).

* Place the second cake disk on top (10).

* Evenly spread a thin layer of the pastry cream on top (11).

* Hull the remaining whole strawberries then set them on top of the cake, pointed ends up (12).

* Scrape the remaining pastry cream into a pastry bag fitted with a ⅓-in (8-mm) plain pastry tube and pipe pointed mounds of cream on top of the cake between the strawberries (13) to (14).

* Refrigerate overnight (15). Just before serving, carefully remove the ring.

4

5

6

7

8

9

10

11

12

13

14

15

Tout-Choco

CHOCOLATE MOUSSE LAYER CAKE

★ ★ ★

SERVES
6 to 8

PREPARATION TIME: 1 hour · REFRIGERATION TIME: 3 hours, plus overnight · COOKING TIME: 32 minutes
One 6-in (16-cm) square cake ring or one 7-in (18-cm) round cake ring

FOR THE COCOA SABLÉ: ⅓ cup plus 1 tbsp plus ½ tsp (1½ oz/40 g) all-purpose flour · 3 tbsp
(1 oz/25 g) almond flour · ¼ cup (1 oz/25 g) hazelnut flour · 1 tsp (¹⁄₁₀ oz/2 g) unsweetened cocoa
powder, sifted · 3 tbsp plus 1¾ tsp (1¾ oz/50 g) unsalted butter, room temperature · ¼ cup minus
1 tsp (1¾ oz/50 g) light brown sugar
FOR THE CHOCOLATE CREAM: 2 large (1⅓ oz/38 g) egg yolks · 2 tbsp (1 oz/25 g) granulated
sugar · ¼ cup plus 2 ½ tbsp (100 mL) whole milk · ¾ cup plus 1½ tbsp (200 mL) heavy whipping
cream · 4 ½ oz (130 g) premium couverture dark chocolate, in disks or evenly chopped
FOR THE CHOCOLATE SPONGE CAKE: 1¾ oz (50 g) premium couverture dark chocolate, in disks or
evenly chopped · 3 tbsp plus 1¾ tsp (1¾ oz/50 g) unsalted butter, room temperature · 3 tbsp plus
1 tsp (¾ oz/20 g) all-purpose flour · 1 tbsp (⅓ oz/10 g) cornstarch · 2 large (2⅛ oz/60 g)
egg whites · ¼ cup (1¾ oz/50 g) granulated sugar
FOR THE CHOCOLATE MOUSSE: 1 (¹⁄₁₀ oz/3 g) gelatin sheet, or 1 tsp (¹⁄₁₀ oz/3 g) powdered gelatin ·
3 large (2 oz/57 g) egg yolks · ¼ cup (60 mL) whole milk · ¼ cup (60 mL) heavy whipping cream ·
1 tbsp (15 mL) very warm water · 4 ¼ oz (120 g) premium couverture dark chocolate, in disks or
evenly chopped · 1 large (1 oz/30 g) egg white · ¼ cup plus 2 ½ tsp (2⅛ oz/60 g) granulated
sugar · ¼ cup plus 2 ½ tbsp (100 mL) heavy whipping cream, well chilled
FOR THE GLAZE: 1 ½ (⅛ oz/5 g) gelatin sheets, or 1 ½ tsp (⅛ oz/5 g) powdered gelatin · 1 tbsp
(15 mL) very warm water · 3 tbsp (45 mL) heavy whipping cream · ¼ cup plus 1 ¼ tsp (2 oz/55 g)
granulated sugar · 1 tbsp (¼ oz/6 g) unsweetened cocoa powder, sifted
FOR THE DECORATION: Chocolate curls or shavings

* Make the cocoa sablé. In a large mixing bowl, whisk the all-purpose, almond, and hazelnut flours and the cocoa powder. In a separate bowl, thoroughly combine the butter and brown sugar with a spoon, then incorporate the flour mixture. Refrigerate for at least 1 hour.

* Preheat the oven to 300°F/150°C. Line a baking sheet with parchment paper.

* Evenly spread the dough about ⅛ in (3 mm) thick onto the prepared baking sheet (the batter should be slightly larger than the cake ring that will be used for assembly). Bake for 12 minutes. Cool completely. Carefully remove the parchment paper from the cocoa sablé.

* Make the chocolate cream. In a medium bowl, vigorously whisk together the egg yolks and sugar until lightened.

* In a saucepan, warm the milk with the cream. Slowly pour the milk mixture into the egg mixture while whisking constantly. Pour the combined mixture back into the saucepan

Tout-Choco
CHOCOLATE MOUSSE LAYER CAKE

and cook over very low heat, stirring constantly, until the mixture coats the back of the spoon, about 5 minutes. Place the chocolate in a separate bowl and pour the cream over the top. Whisk until smooth. Let cool slightly. Using an immersion blender, blend the mixture until smooth. Cool completely.

* Make the chocolate sponge cake. Preheat the oven to 375°F/190°C. Place the cake ring on a baking sheet lined with parchment paper.

* In a large heatproof bowl set over a pot of simmering water, melt the chocolate and butter together (or place them in a microwave-safe bowl and microwave for 1 minute), then stir until completely melted. Sift together the flour and cornstarch. Beat the egg whites into stiff peaks, adding the sugar a little at a time halfway through the beating time. Add the flour mixture to the melted chocolate and stir just until combined. Carefully fold in the beaten egg whites. Scrape the batter into the prepared ring, gently spreading it out evenly. Bake for 10 minutes. Cool completely.

* Assemble the Tout-Choco. Make the chocolate mousse. Soak the gelatin sheet for 10 minutes in a bowl of cold water. (If using powdered gelatin, sprinkle it over 1 tbsp plus 2 tsp (25 mL) cold water and stir to moisten it; let soften for 5 minutes.)

* In a small bowl, lightly whisk the egg yolks. In a small saucepan, heat the milk with the cream. Slowly pour the milk mixture into the egg mixture while whisking constantly. Pour the combined mixture back into the saucepan and cook over very low heat, stirring constantly, until the mixture coats the back of the spoon, about 5 minutes.

* Squeeze the water from the gelatin sheet and add it to the warm water; stir to dissolve. Stir the gelatin mixture into the warm custard (or stir in the softened powdered gelatin, if using, until fully melted). Let cool slightly.

* Place the chocolate in a large bowl and pour the warm custard mixture over the top then whisk until smooth. Let cool.

* In a heatproof bowl set over a pot of simmering water, gently heat the egg whites and sugar, whisking constantly. Once the sugar has dissolved, remove from the heat. Whip the egg whites and sugar into stiff peaks. In a separate bowl, whip the cream.

* Fold the meringue, and then the whipped cream, into the chocolate mixture. Trim the cocoa sablé to the size of the cake ring. Place the ring on a serving plate and place the chocolate sponge layer in the bottom of the ring. Add a thin layer (about ¼ in/6 mm) of chocolate mousse on top of the cake and spread it out evenly.

* Cover the mousse with the chocolate cream. Add the remaining mousse and smooth the top. Refrigerate for at least 2 hours.

* Make the glaze. Soak the gelatin sheets for 10 minutes in a bowl of cold water. (If using powdered gelatin, sprinkle it over 2½ tbsp (40 mL) cold water and stir to moisten it; let soften for 5 minutes.) Squeeze the water from the gelatin sheets and add them to the warm water; stir to dissolve.

* In a small saucepan, heat the cream, sugar, and 1 tbsp (15 mL) water. Stir in the gelatin mixture (or stir in the softened powdered gelatin, if using, until fully melted) and the cocoa. Using an immersion blender, blend until smooth. Pour a thin layer of the glaze over the top of cake while still in the ring. Refrigerate until the next day.

* Just before serving, remove the ring and decorate the cake with chocolate shavings or curls.

Charlotte aux Framboises

RASPBERRY MOUSSE CAKE

★ ★ ★

SERVES
6 to 8

PREPARATION TIME: 45 minutes · COOKING TIME: 12 minutes · REFRIGERATION TIME: Overnight
One 7-in (18-cm) to 8-in (20-cm) round cake ring

FOR THE LADYFINGERS: 1⅓ cups (4½ oz/130 g) all-purpose flour · 3 large (3⅛ oz/90 g) egg whites · ½ cup plus 1 tbsp plus ½ tsp (4 oz/115 g) granulated sugar · 7 large (4⅔ oz/133 g) egg yolks · ½ cup (1¾ oz/50 g) confectioners' sugar

FOR THE RASPBERRY MOUSSE: · 3 (⅓ oz/9 g) gelatin sheets, or 1 tbsp (⅓ oz/9 g) powdered gelatin · 1 tbsp (15 mL) very warm water · 1⅓ cups (10½ oz/300 g) store-bought raspberry purée · 1½ tbsp (22 mL) freshly squeezed lemon juice (from ½ lemon) · 1⅓ cups (300 mL) heavy whipping cream, well chilled

FOR THE ITALIAN MERINGUE: ½ cup plus 2 tbsp plus 1¼ tsp (4½ oz/130 g) granulated sugar · 2 large (2⅛ oz/60 g) egg whites

FOR THE DECORATION: 2 pints (16 oz/452 g) fresh raspberries · ¼ cup (1 oz/25 g) confectioners' sugar

* Make the ladyfingers. Preheat the oven to 350°F/180°C.

* Sift the flour ①.

* In the bowl of a standing mixer fitted with the whisk attachment, beat the egg whites into stiff peaks, adding the sugar a little at a time halfway through the beating time ②.

* Reduce the speed to low, add the egg yolks, and beat until incorporated ③.

* Transfer the mixture to a bowl. Carefully fold in the flour, just until incorporated ④ to ⑤.

* On a large piece of parchment paper, draw two parallel lines 25½ in (65 cm) long and 2¾ in (7 cm) apart. Invert the paper; the lines should be visible through the paper ⑥.

* Using a pastry bag fitted with a ⅓-in (8-mm) plain pastry tube, pipe side-by-side "fingers" of batter between the two parallel lines ⑦.

* Sift some of the confectioners' sugar over the top of the fingers, twice, at 15-minute intervals ⑧.

* On a separate sheet of parchment paper, draw two circles using a template (such as another cake ring) that is ¾ in (2 cm) smaller than the cake ring in which the cake will be assembled ⑨. Invert the paper; the lines should be visible through the paper.

* Using the outline of the circles as a guide, pipe two disks of batter, starting in the center and moving out in a spiral pattern to the edge ⑩.

* Sift confectioners' sugar over the top of the disks, twice, at 15-minute intervals ⑪.

Charlotte aux Framboises
RASPBERRY MOUSSE CAKE

* Bake for 9 minutes.
* Make the raspberry mousse. Soak the gelatin sheets for 10 minutes in a bowl of cold water. (If using powdered gelatin, sprinkle it over ¼ cup plus 1 tbsp (75 mL) cold water and stir to moisten it; let soften for 5 minutes.) Squeeze the water from the gelatin sheets and add them to the warm water; stir to dissolve.
* In a saucepan, warm the raspberry purée, then stir in the gelatin mixture (or stir in the softened powdered gelatin, if using, until fully melted) and the lemon juice. Let cool slightly (12) to (14).
* Whip the cream, then fold it into the purée mixture (15).
* Make the Italian meringue following the step-by-step instructions in the Opéra recipe on page 154. In a small heavy saucepan, heat the sugar and 1 tbsp (15 mL) water over high heat to 250°F/ 121°C (if you do not have a candy thermometer, drop a small quantity of the hot syrup into a bowl of cold water. It should form a ball and feel soft when pinched between your fingers).
* Meanwhile, using a standing or handheld mixer, begin beating the egg whites until soft peaks form. When the syrup reaches 250°F/121°C, pour it in a steady stream down the inside edge of the bowl with the mixer on medium speed and continue beating until all of the syrup is incorporated and the egg whites are stiff and glossy.
* Fold the meringue into the whipped cream-purée mixture (16).
* Assemble the raspberry Charlotte (17). Place the cake ring on a serving plate and line the edges with the ladyfingers (flat sides in), trimming off any overlapping portion (18).
* Place one of the ladyfinger disks at the bottom of the ring (19).
* Scrape in half of the mousse (20).
* Distribute some of the raspberries on top of the mousse (set aside the most attractive ones for the top) (21).
* Cover them with the second ladyfinger disk, pressing down lightly to evenly set the disk (22) to (23).
* Cover the disk with the remaining mousse and spread it out evenly (24).
* Place the remaining raspberries on top (25).
* Dust with confectioners' sugar (26). Refrigerate overnight.

(4)

(5)

(6)

7

8

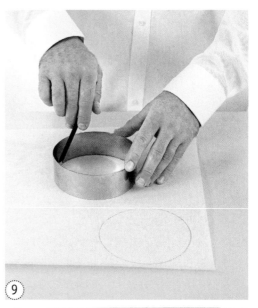

9

10

11

12

13

14

15

Charlotte aux Framboises

RASPBERRY MOUSSE CAKE

Macarons

MERINGUE SANDWICH COOKIES

Macarons

MERINGUE SANDWICH COOKIES

★ ★ ★

MAKES 8 INDIVIDUAL MACARONS, 3 DOZEN SMALL MACARONS, OR 1 MACARONNADE

PREPARATION TIME: 2 hours • COOKING TIME: 16 minutes

BASE RECIPE FOR THE SHELLS: 4 or 5 large (4 oz/115 g) egg whites • 1 cup plus 2 tbsp (5 ½ oz/155 g) almond flour • 1½ cups plus 1 tbsp plus 2 tsp (5 ½ oz/160 g) confectioners' sugar • Flavoring (according to the recipe) • ¾ cup plus 2 ½ tsp (5 ½ oz/160 g) granulated sugar • Powdered food color (according to the recipe; optional)

* Separate the yolks and the whites of 4 or 5 eggs and weigh the whites to exactly 4 oz (115 g) (1).

* Divide the whites evenly between two bowls.

* In a large bowl, sift together the almond flour and confectioners' sugar (2).

* Add one of the bowls of egg whites to the almond flour mixture along with any flavoring indicated in the recipe (3).

* Mix vigorously with a silicone spatula (4).

* Add the sugar, food color (if using), and 3 tbsp (45 mL) water to a small saucepan. Heat over high heat to 250°F/121°C (if you do not have a candy thermometer, drop a small quantity of the hot syrup into a bowl of cold water. It should form a ball and feel soft when pinched between your fingers) (5).

* Meanwhile, in the bowl of a standing mixer fitted with the whisk attachment, begin beating the remaining egg whites until soft peaks form. When the syrup reaches 250°F/121°C, pour it in a steady stream down the inside edge of the bowl with the mixer on medium speed (6).

* Adjust the color, if necessary, by adding more food color (the intensity of the color varies by brand). Continue beating for several minutes on low speed until the whites are stiff and glossy (7).

* Incorporate a small amount of the meringue into the almond flour mixture to lighten it (8).

* Incorporate the remaining meringue while energetically folding the batter for several minutes to deflate it. It should fall back into the bowl in the form of a ribbon when the spatula is raised (this step is called *macaronner*) (9).

Note: The step-by-step photos represent a tripled recipe.

Macarons

MERINGUE SANDWICH COOKIES

* Pipe the shells. Line a baking sheet with parchment paper. Scrape the batter into a pastry bag fitted with a 1/3-in (10-mm) plain pastry tube  10 .

* For small macarons, pipe shells 1 1/8 in (3 cm) to 1 1/2 in (4 cm) in diameter 11 .

* For individual macarons, pipe shells 2 1/4 in (6 cm) to 2 3/4 in (7 cm) in diameter 12 .

* For the large macaronnade shells, using a plate as a template, draw two 7-in (18-cm) circles on parchment paper. This size will serve six 13 .

* Invert the paper (the lines should be visible through the paper) then pipe the macaron batter in a spiral, starting from the center, without any gaps between the lines 14 .

* For a heart-shaped macaronnade shell, fold a piece of paper and cut out a half-heart shape to use as a template—the unfolded heart should fit inside a rectangle measuring about 8 in (20 cm) by 4 in (10 cm)—and use it to trace two hearts onto parchment paper. 15 .

* Invert the paper (the lines should be visible through the paper), then pipe the macaron batter to fill the inside of the template, starting from the edge and working in toward the center 16 .

* Let the piped shells sit at room temperature for 1 hour to allow a skin to form (the batter should not feel sticky when lightly touched with your finger).

* Meanwhile, preheat the oven to 250°F/ 125°C. Bake for 16 minutes (the shells should not begin to brown).

13

14

15

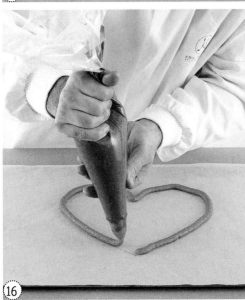

16

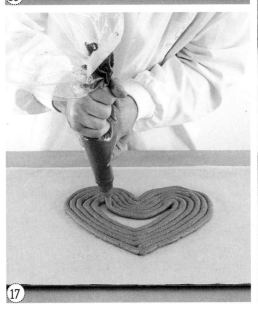

17

Macarons à la Vanille ou au Chocolat

VANILLA OR CHOCOLATE MERINGUE SANDWICH COOKIES

MAKES 8 INDIVIDUAL MACARONS OR 36 SMALL MACARONS

PREPARATION TIME: 20 minutes (not including the shells) · COOKING TIME: 16 minutes · REFRIGERATION TIME: Overnight

Vanilla Meringue Sandwich Cookies

FOR THE VANILLA SHELLS: 4 or 5 large (4 oz/115 g) egg whites · 1 cup plus 2 tbsp (5½ oz/155 g) almond flour · 1½ cups (5¼ oz/150 g) confectioners' sugar · ¼ tsp (0.5 g) vanilla powder · ¾ cup plus 2½ tsp (5½ oz/160 g) granulated sugar

FOR THE VANILLA GANACHE: 1 tsp (1/10 oz/3 g) cornstarch · ½ cup plus 1 tbsp (133 mL) heavy whipping cream, divided · 1¾ oz (50 g) premium couverture white chocolate, in disks or evenly chopped · 1 tsp (5 mL) pure vanilla extract · ¼ cup (1¾ oz/50 g) granulated sugar · ½ stick plus 1¾ tsp (2⅓ oz/65 g) unsalted butter

Chocolate Meringue Sandwich Cookies

FOR CHOCOLATE THE SHELLS: 4 or 5 large (4 oz/115 g) egg whites · ⅓ cup plus 1 tsp (1 oz/30 g) unsweetened cocoa powder · 1 cup plus 1 tbsp (5⅛ oz (145 g) almond flour · 1½ cups minus 2 tsp (5⅛ oz/145 g) confectioners' sugar · ¼ tsp (0.5 g) vanilla powder · ¾ cup plus 2½ tsp (5½ oz/160 g) granulated sugar · 1 small pinch powdered carmine red food color (optional)

FOR THE CHOCOLATE GANACHE: 6⅓ oz (180 g) premium couverture dark chocolate, in disks or evenly chopped · ¾ cup (180 mL) heavy whipping cream · 1 tbsp plus 1¾ tsp (¾ oz/20 g) granulated sugar

* Make the shells, following the step-by-step instructions on page 176 (for the chocolate macarons, sifting together the cocoa, almond flour, confectioners' sugar, and vanilla powder).

* Make the vanilla ganache. In a small bowl, combine the cornstarch with 1 tbsp (15 mL) of the cream. Place the chocolate in a large bowl. In a heavy saucepan, heat the remaining cream with the vanilla and sugar until hot, then pour the cream mixture over the chocolate. Let sit for several minutes. Stir in the cornstarch mixture, then the butter until very smooth. Cool completely.

* Transfer the ganache to a pastry bag fitted with a ⅓-in (8-mm) plain pastry tube. Turn half of the shells over with the flat sides up onto a piece of parchment paper. Fill them with the ganache. Cover them with another shell, pressing down gently.

* Refrigerate for at least 24 hours in an airtight container before serving.

Variation: Make the chocolate ganache. Place the chocolate in a large bowl. In a heavy saucepan, heat the cream with the sugar until hot, then pour the cream mixture over the chocolate. Let sit for several minutes, then whisk until smooth. Cool completely.

Macarons au Citron et á la Menthe

LEMON-MINT MERINGUE SANDWICH COOKIES

★ ★ ★

MAKES 8 INDIVIDUAL MACARONS OR 36 MINI MACARONS

PREPARATION TIME: 25 minutes (not including the shells) · COOKING TIME: 16 minutes · REFRIGERATION TIME: 3 hours, plus overnight

FOR THE SHELLS: 4 or 5 large (4 oz/115 g) egg whites · 1 cup plus 2 tbsp (5 ½ oz/155 g) almond flour · 1 ½ cups (5 ¼ oz/150 g) confectioners' sugar · ¾ cup plus 2 ½ tsp (5 ½ oz/160 g) granulated sugar · 1 small pinch powdered lemon yellow food color · 1 small pinch powdered green food color
FOR THE LEMON-MINT CREAM: 2 large (3 ½ oz/100 g) eggs · ½ cup (3 ½ oz/100 g) granulated sugar · 1 tbsp (⅓ oz/10 g) cornstarch · ⅓ cup (80 mL) freshly squeezed lemon juice, including the pulp (from 2 lemons) · ⅓ (1 g) gelatin sheet, or ⅓ tsp (1 g) powdered gelatin · 1 tbsp (15 mL) very warm water · 2 or 3 drops mint extract (quantity will be determined by the intensity of flavor) · 1 stick plus 1 tbsp (4 ½ oz/130 g) unsalted butter, chilled and cut into pieces

* Make the shells following the step-by-step instructions on page 176, adding yellow food color to half of the batter and green food color to the other half.

* Make the lemon-mint cream. In a large bowl, whisk together the eggs, sugar, and cornstarch.

* In a small heavy saucepan, bring the lemon juice to a boil, then whisk in the egg mixture.

* Bring the mixture to a boil again, stirring constantly, and cook until very thick, about 5 minutes.

* Soak the gelatin sheet for 10 minutes in a bowl of cold water. (If using powdered gelatin, sprinkle it over 2 tsp (10 mL) cold water and stir to moisten it; let soften for 5 minutes.) Squeeze the water from the gelatin sheet and add it to

the warm water; stir to dissolve. Stir the gelatin mixture into the warm custard (or stir in the softened powdered gelatin, if using, until fully melted). Stir in the mint extract. Let cool slightly.

* Add the butter pieces to the custard. Using an immersion blender, blend the mixture until smooth and the butter is incorporated. Cover the surface with plastic wrap then refrigerate for at least 3 hours.

* Scrape the cream into a pastry bag fitted with a ⅓-in (8-mm) plain pastry tube. Turn the green shells over with the flat sides up onto a piece of parchment paper and fill them with the cream. Cover them with the yellow shells, pressing down gently.

* Refrigerate for at least 24 hours in an airtight container before serving.

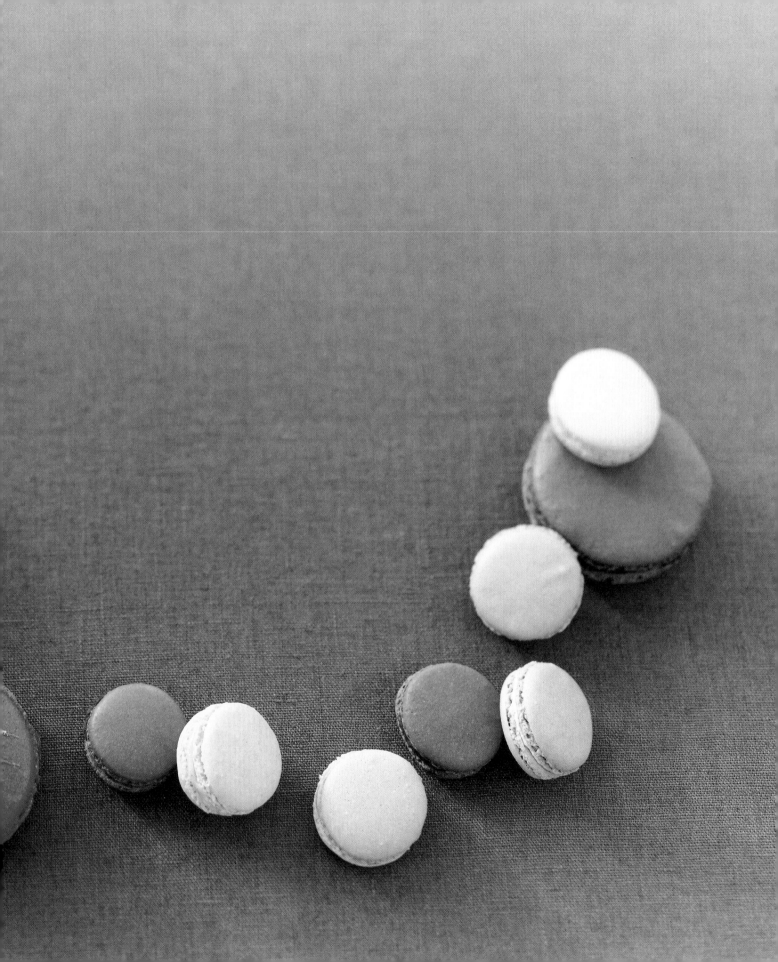

Macarons à la Framboise et au Citron Vert

RASPBERRY-LIME MERINGUE SANDWICH COOKIES

MAKES 8 INDIVIDUAL MACARONS OR 36 MINI MACARONS

PREPARATION TIME: 15 minutes (not including the shells) · COOKING TIME: 16 minutes · REFRIGERATION TIME: Overnight

FOR THE SHELLS: 4 or 5 large (4 oz/115 g) egg whites · 1 cup plus 2 tbsp (5 ½ oz/155 g) almond flour · 1 ½ cups (5 ¼ oz/160 g) confectioners' sugar · ¾ cup plus 2 ½ tsp (5 ½ oz/160 g) granulated sugar · 1 or 2 pinches powdered raspberry red food color (intensity of color will depend on brand and your color preference)

FOR THE RASPBERRY-LIME FILLING: 9 ½ oz (270 g) raspberry preserves with a firm consistency (preferably with seeds) · ¼ cup plus 2 tsp (1 ½ oz/40 g) almond flour · 1 tsp (1/10 oz/2 g) freshly grated lime zest (from ½ lime)

FOR THE DECORATION: 3 ½ oz (100 g) premium couverture white chocolate, in disks or evenly chopped · 2 or 3 drops liquid green food color

* Make the shells, following the step-by-step instructions on page 176.

* Make the raspberry-lime filling. In a large bowl, combine the preserves, almond flour, and zest.

* Make the decoration. In a heatproof bowl set over a pot of simmering water, melt the chocolate over very low heat without stirring (or place it in a microwave-safe bowl and microwave for 1 minute). Stir briefly, then add the food color and stir to combine well. Pour the colored chocolate into a small paper cone, then lightly stripe the tops of the macaron shells with it in a zigzag pattern.

* Scrape the filling into a pastry bag fitted with a 1/3-in (8-mm) pastry tube. Turn half of the shells over with the flat sides up onto a piece of parchment paper and fill them with the filling. Cover them with another shell, pressing down gently.

* Refrigerate for at least 24 hours in an airtight container before serving.

Macarons á la Pistache

PISTACHIO MERINGUE SANDWICH COOKIES

★★★

MAKES 8 INDIVIDUAL MACARONS OR 36 MINI MACARONS

PREPARATION TIME: 25 minutes (not including the shells) · COOKING TIME: 16 minutes
REFRIGERATION TIME: Overnight

FOR THE SHELLS: 4 or 5 large (4 oz/115 g) egg whites · 1 cup (5 oz/140 g) almond flour · ⅓ cup (2 oz/55 g) pistachio flour · 1¾ cups (6⅛ oz/175 g) confectioners' sugar · ¾ cup plus 2½ tsp (5½ oz/160 g) granulated sugar · 1 or 2 pinches powdered pistachio green food color (intensity of color will depend on brand and your color preference)

FOR THE PISTACHIO CREAM: 2 tbsp plus 1¼ tsp (1 oz/30 g) granulated sugar · 1 large (1¾ oz/50 g) egg · 1 stick minus ¾ tsp (3¾ oz/110 g) unsalted butter, room temperature · 1 oz (30 g) pistachio paste · ½ cup minus 2 tsp (2⅓ oz/65 g) almond flour · ½ cup plus 2 tbsp plus 1 tsp (2⅓ oz/65 g) confectioners' sugar, sifted

* Make the shells, following the step-by-step instructions on page 176, whisking together the almond and pistachio flours.

* Make the pistachio cream. In a small heavy saucepan, heat the sugar and 1 tbsp (15 mL) water over high heat to 250°F/121°C (if you do not have a candy thermometer, drop a small quantity of the hot syrup into a bowl of cold water. It should form a ball and feel soft when pinched between your fingers).

* Meanwhile, using a handheld mixer, begin beating the egg. As soon as the syrup reaches 250°F/121°C, pour it in a steady stream down the inside edge of the bowl with the mixer on medium speed, and continue beating until all of the syrup is incorporated and the mixture is thick and glossy. Reduce the speed to low, and beat in the butter, then the pistachio paste, almond flour, and confectioners' sugar until smooth. Cool completely.

* Scrape the cream into a pastry bag fitted with a ⅓-in (8-mm) plain pastry tube. Turn half of the shells over with the flat sides up onto a piece of parchment paper and fill them with the cream. Cover them with another shell, pressing down gently.

* Refrigerate for at least 24 hours in an airtight container before serving.

Macaronnade

MERINGUE SANDWICH CAKE

★★★

SERVES
6 to 8

PREPARATION TIME: 25 minutes (not including the shells) · COOKING TIME: 16 minutes
REFRIGERATION TIME: 2 hours, plus overnight

FOR THE SHELLS: 4 or 5 large (4 oz/115 g) egg whites · 1 cup plus 2 tbsp (5 ½ oz/155 g) almond flour · 1½ cups plus 1 tbsp plus 2 tsp (5 ½ oz/160 g) confectioners' sugar · ¾ cup plus 2 ½ tsp (5 ½ oz/160 g) granulated sugar · 1 small pinch powdered raspberry red food color

FOR THE PISTACHIO PASTRY CREAM: 1¾ cups plus 2 tbsp (450 mL) whole milk · ½ cup plus 2 ½ tsp (3 ¾ oz/110 g) granulated sugar · ¼ cup plus ¾ tbsp (1½ oz/45 g) cornstarch · 3 large (2 oz/57 g) egg yolks · 1 oz (25 g) pistachio paste · ⅔ cup (150 mL) heavy whipping cream, well chilled · 3 pints (1½ lb/680 g) fresh raspberries

FOR THE DECORATION (OPTIONAL): 1 sheet edible gold leaf

* Make the macaron shells following the step-by-step instructions on page 176. Pipe two 8 ½-in (22-cm) disks and bake them for 16 minutes ①.

* Make the pistachio pastry cream following the step-by-step instructions on page 138 incorporating the pistachio paste. Refrigerate for at least 2 hours.

* Whip the cream then fold it into the pastry cream using a silicone spatula or whisk ② to ③.

* Place one macaron shell upside down on a serving plate (select the more attractive of the two disks for the top shell). Scrape the pastry cream into a pastry bag fitted with a large plain pastry tube and pipe the cream in a spiral pattern on top of the disk, leaving about a ¾-in (2-cm) border for the raspberries ④ to ⑤.

* Place the most attractive raspberries around the edge of the disk (set aside several raspberries for the top decoration) ⑥.

* Place the least attractive raspberries in the center on top of the cream ⑦, then cover them with a thin layer of the cream ⑧.

* Place the second disk on top ⑨.

* Pipe small dabs of pastry cream randomly on top of the disk to help secure the raspberries on the top shell ⑩.

* Set the raspberries on top of the dabs of cream ⑪.

* Refrigerate for at least 24 hours in an airtight container before serving.

Note: For special occasions, you can place edible gold leaf on top. Delicately pick up the gold leaf with the point of a knife and place it in random spots on top of the raspberries ⑫. Be careful, as the smallest breeze can carry the gold leaf away as easily as a feather!

You can also carefully dip the bottom of the raspberries used for decoration in confectioners' sugar before placing them on top of the dabs of cream.

Macaronnade

MERINGUE SANDWICH CAKE

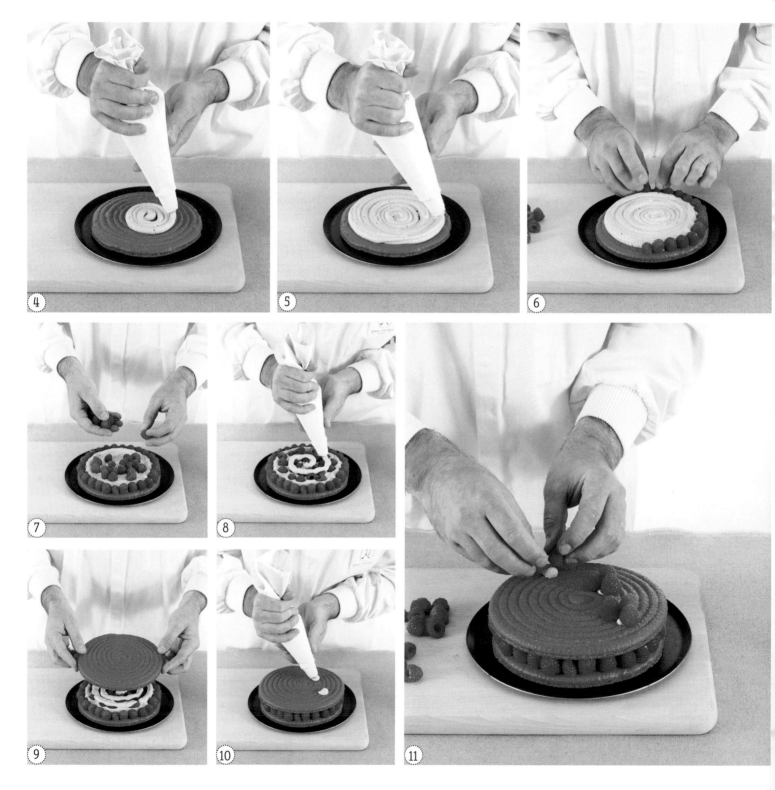

COFFEE YULE LOG

★★★

SERVES
6 to 8

PREPARATION TIME: 45 minutes · COOKING TIME: 15 minutes

FOR THE COFFEE SYRUP: ½ cup (3½ oz/100 g) granulated sugar · ½ tsp (3 mL) coffee extract · 1 tsp (1/10 oz/2 g) instant coffee

FOR THE SPONGE CAKE: 1⅓ cups (4½ oz/130 g) all-purpose flour · 3 large (3⅛ oz/90 g) egg whites · ½ cup plus 1 tbsp plus ½ tsp (4 oz/115 g) granulated sugar · 7 large (4⅔ oz/133 g) egg yolks

FOR THE ITALIAN MERINGUE: ¼ cup plus 2½ tsp (2⅛ oz/60 g) granulated sugar · 1 large (1 oz/30 g) egg white

FOR THE COFFEE BUTTERCREAM: 3 tbsp plus 1 tsp (50 mL) whole milk · 1 tsp (1/10 oz/2 g) coarsely crushed coffee beans · 1 large (⅔ oz/19 g) egg yolk · 1 tbsp plus 1¾ tsp (¾ oz/20 g) granulated sugar · 1 tsp (1/10 oz/2 g) instant coffee · 1 stick plus 3 tbsp plus 1 tsp (5½ oz160 g) unsalted butter, room temperature

FOR THE DECORATION: Chocolate-covered coffee beans

∗ Have ready a 9½-in (24-cm) by 3-in (8-cm) cardboard base to facilitate slicing the sponge cake.

∗ Make the coffee syrup. In a saucepan, combine the sugar with a ¼ cup plus 2½ tbsp (100 mL) water and bring to a boil. Add the coffee extract and instant coffee and stir to combine. Set aside, covered.

∗ Preheat the oven to 350°F/180°C. Line a rimmed sheet pan with parchment paper.

∗ Make the sponge cake, following the step-by-step instructions for the Charlotte ladyfingers recipe on page 168, but do not pipe the fingers. Sift the flour. In the bowl of a standing mixer fitted with the whisk attachment, beat the egg whites into stiff peaks, adding the sugar a little at a time halfway through the beating time.

∗ Reduce the speed to low, add the egg yolks, and beat until incorporated. Transfer the mixture to a bowl and carefully fold in the flour, just until incorporated. Spread the batter evenly into the prepared sheet pan and bake for 10 minutes.

Bûche au Café

COFFEE YULE LOG

* Make the Italian meringue. In a small heavy saucepan, heat the sugar and 1 tbsp (15 mL) water over high heat to 250°F/121°C (if you do not have a candy thermometer, drop a small quantity of the hot syrup into a bowl of cold water. It should form a ball and feel soft when pinched between your fingers).

* Meanwhile, using a handheld mixer, begin beating the egg white until soft peaks form. When the syrup reaches 250°F/121°C, pour it in a steady stream down the inside edge of the bowl with the mixer on medium speed, and continue beating until all of the syrup is incorporated and the egg white is stiff and glossy.

* Make the coffee buttercream. In a small saucepan, bring the milk to a boil, then add the crushed coffee beans to infuse. Let cool, then strain through a fine-mesh strainer. In a large bowl, whisk together the egg yolk and the sugar. Reheat the infused milk then whisk it into the egg mixture. Pour the entire mixture back into the saucepan. Add the instant coffee and cook over very low heat, stirring constantly, until the mixture coats the back of the spoon, about 5 minutes. Let cool.

* In the bowl of a standing mixer fitted with the whisk attachment, beat the butter until creamy. Beat in the cooked cream a little at a time until incorporated. Fold this mixture into the Italian meringue.

* Assemble the Coffee Yule Log 1. Cut out a 9½-in (24-cm) by 15¾-in (40-cm) rectangle from the sponge cake using the cardboard base as a template 2.

* Place it on top of a large piece of parchment paper or a clean kitchen towel.

* Brush the cake with the coffee syrup using a pastry brush 3 to 4.

* Spread half of the buttercream evenly on top 5 to 6.

* Tightly roll the cake, using the parchment paper (or the towel) to assist you 7.

* Use the piece of cardboard to press the parchment paper securely against the cake to keep it tightly rolled 8.

* Place the log on a rectangular cake board 9 and pipe two large dabs of cream (in the photo vanilla buttercream is used, but you can also use the coffee buttercream from this recipe) to resemble detachment points of branches 10.

* Place the remaining buttercream in a pastry bag, preferably fitted with a flat yule log pastry tube (see Specialized Equipment, page viii), and pipe flat ribbons of buttercream to cover the cake 11.

* To achieve a more rustic "bark" appearance, use a fork to score the buttercream.

* Place chocolate-covered coffee beans on top for decoration 12.

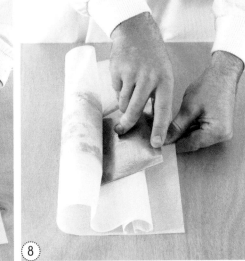

Bûche Forêt-Noire

BLACK FOREST YULE LOG

★ ★ ★

SERVES
8 to 10

PREPARATION TIME: 1 hour (over 2 days) • COOKING TIME: 10 minutes • FREEZING TIME: 3 hours, plus overnight
One 12-in (30-cm) yule log mold (see Specialized Equipment, page viii) and a rigid rectangular cake board
the same length and width as the inside of the mold (see Variation)

FOR THE COCOA SPONGE CAKE: ¼ cup plus ½ tsp (1 oz/25 g) all-purpose flour • ¼ cup plus 2 tsp (1½ oz/40 g) almond flour • ⅓ cup
minus 2 tsp (1 oz/25 g) unsweetened cocoa powder • 1 tbsp plus 2 tsp (1 oz/25 g) unsalted butter • 1 large (1¾ oz/50 g) egg • 1 large
(⅔ oz/19 g) egg yolk • ½ cup (3½ oz/100 g) granulated sugar, divided • 3 large (3⅛ oz/90 g) egg whites
FOR THE CHERRY CENTER: ¼ cup plus 2½ tsp (2⅛ oz/60 g) granulated sugar • 3 tbsp (45 mL) Morello cherry syrup (reserved from the
cherries) • 1½ cups (350 mL) heavy whipping cream, well chilled • ¼ cup plus 2 tsp (1 oz/30 g) confectioners' sugar, sifted • 5¼ oz (150 g)
pitted Morello cherries in kirsch (cherry liqueur), well drained (reserve liquid)
FOR THE CHOCOLATE MOUSSE: ¼ cup plus 1 tbsp plus 1¾ tsp (2½ oz/70 g) granulated sugar • 4 large (2⅔ oz/76 g) egg yolks •
9 oz (250 g) premium couverture dark chocolate, in disks or evenly chopped • 1½ cups (350 mL) heavy whipping cream, well chilled
FOR THE GLAZE: 1½ (⅛ oz/5 g) gelatin sheets, or 1½ tsp (⅛ oz/5 g) powdered gelatin • 1 tbsp (15 mL) very warm water • 3 tbsp (45 mL)
heavy whipping cream • ¼ cup plus 1¼ tsp (2 oz/55 g) granulated sugar • 1 tbsp (¼ oz/6 g) unsweetened cocoa powder, sifted
FOR THE DECORATION: Chocolate shavings or squares (optional) • Morello cherries in kirsch with the stems, dipped in chocolate (optional)

⁎ The day before serving, make the cocoa sponge cake. Preheat the oven to 325°F/160°C. Line a rimmed sheet pan with
parchment paper.

⁎ Sift together the all-purpose and almond flours and the cocoa. Melt the butter. Let it cool slightly, but remain liquid. In
the bowl of a standing mixer fitted with the whisk attachment,

beat the egg and egg yolk with half the sugar until lightened, then beat in the melted butter. Beat the egg whites into stiff peaks, adding the remaining sugar a little at a time halfway through the beating time. Fold the meringue into the egg yolk mixture using a silicone spatula. Gently fold in the flour mixture.

* Spread the batter evenly onto the prepared pan. Increase the oven temperature to 350°F/180°C and bake for 10 minutes.

* Cool completely. Carefully peel the parchment paper from the bottom of the cake. Cut out two 11-in (28-cm)-long rectangles slightly narrower than the width of the mold. Wrap tightly in plastic wrap and refrigerate until ready to assemble the cake

* Make the cherry center. In a small saucepan, bring the granulated sugar, cherry syrup, and 3 tbsp (45 mL) water to a boil. Set aside, covered, to cool.

* Line the bottom and the sides of the yule log mold with plastic wrap. Place one of the cake rectangles inside the mold and brush it with the cherry syrup using a pastry brush. Beat the cream into soft peaks, slowly adding the confectioners' sugar halfway through the beating time.

* Cover the cake with a thick layer of whipped cream, then carefully push the cherries down into it. Cover the cream layer with the second strip of cake and brush it with the syrup. Fold the ends of the plastic wrap over the center and freeze for at least 3 hours.

* The next day, assemble the cake. Make the chocolate mousse. In a small heavy saucepan, heat the sugar and 3 tbsp (45 mL) water over high heat to 250°F/119°C (if you do not have a candy thermometer, drop a small quantity of the hot syrup into a bowl of cold water. It should form a ball and feel soft when pinched between your fingers).

* Meanwhile, using a handheld mixer, begin beating the egg yolks. When the syrup reaches 250°F/119°C, pour it in a steady stream down the inside edge of the bowl with the mixer on medium speed and continue beating until the mixture is smooth and creamy.

* In a large heatproof bowl set over a pot of simmering water, gently melt the chocolate (or place it in a microwave-safe bowl and microwave for 1 minute), then stir until completely melted; let cool slightly.

* Whip the cream. Using a silicone spatula, fold a small amount of the whipped cream into the melted chocolate to lighten it, then fold in the remaining whipped cream. Combine this mixture with the egg mixture.

* Unmold the cherry center and trim the border so that it is tidy and clean and a little narrower than the log mold. Line the sides of the log mold with acetate or plastic wrap. Fill half of the pan with the mousse, then place the cherry center on top, centered (it should be level with the top of the mold). Finish filling the mold with the remaining mousse, then cover with plastic wrap and place the mold in the freezer until the next day.

* Make the glaze. Soak the gelatin sheets for 10 minutes in a bowl of cold water. (If using powdered gelatin, sprinkle it over 2 1/2 tbsp (40 mL) cold water and stir to moisten it; let soften for 5 minutes.) Squeeze the water from the gelatin sheets and add them to the warm water; stir to dissolve. In a small saucepan, heat the cream with 1 tbsp (15 mL) water and the sugar. Stir in the gelatin mixture (or stir in the softened powdered gelatin, if using, until fully melted) and the cocoa. Let cool slightly. Using an immersion blender, blend until smooth.

* Place the cake board on top of a wire rack set over a sheet pan. Unmold the cake onto the cake board. Pour the glaze over the entire surface of the cake to cover completely.

* Refrigerate the cake just until ready to serve. Just before serving, place the decoration on top, if using.

Variation: For other times of year, you can make this cake stacked in layers using a traditional cake ring.

Saint-Valentin

VALENTINE'S DAY RASPBERRY-FILLED MOUSSE CAKE

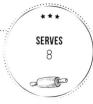

★ ★ ★

SERVES
8

PREPARATION TIME: 1 hour (over 2 days) · FREEZING TIME: 6 hours · COOKING TIME: 10 minutes

One heart-shaped cake ring and one heart-shaped silicone mold about 1 in (2.5 cm) smaller than the cake ring

FOR THE RASPBERRY CENTER: 1⅛ cups (9 oz/250 g) store-bought raspberry purée · ¼ cup plus 2 tbsp (2½ oz/75 g) granulated sugar · 1½ tbsp (22 mL) raspberry liqueur (optional) · 2 (¼ oz/6 g) gelatin sheets, or 2 tsp (¼ oz/6 g) powdered gelatin · 2 tbsp (30 mL) very warm water

FOR THE PLOUGASTEL SPONGE CAKE: 3 tbsp plus 1 tsp (1 oz/30 g) almond flour · 3 large (3⅛ oz/90 g) egg whites, divided · ¼ cup plus 2 tsp (1 oz/30 g) confectioners' sugar, sifted · ¼ cup plus 2½ tsp (2⅛ oz/60 g) granulated sugar · 3 tbsp plus 1 tsp (¾ oz/20 g) all-purpose flour, sifted

FOR THE WHITE CHOCOLATE MOUSSE: 2 large (1⅓ oz/38 g) egg yolks · 3 tbsp (1 oz/30 g) cornstarch · 2 tsp (¼ oz/8 g) granulated sugar · 1 cup plus 2¾ tsp (250 mL) whole milk · 1 (1⁄10 oz/3 g) gelatin sheet, or 1 tsp (1⁄10 oz/3 g) powdered gelatin · 1 tbsp (15 mL) very warm water · 5½ oz (160 g) premium couverture white chocolate, in disks or evenly chopped · ¾ cup plus 1½ tbsp (200 mL) heavy whipping cream, well chilled

FOR THE GLAZE: ⅓ cup (80 mL) heavy whipping cream · ⅓ (1 g) gelatin sheet, or ⅓ tsp (1 g) powdered gelatin · 1 tbsp (15 mL) very warm water · 4¼ oz (120 g) premium couverture white chocolate, in disks or evenly chopped · Several drops liquid red food color

FOR THE DECORATION: Several fresh raspberries

* The day before serving, make the raspberry center. In a saucepan, gently heat the raspberry purée with the sugar, then stir in the liqueur, if using. Soak the gelatin sheets for 10 minutes in a bowl of cold water. (If using powdered gelatin, sprinkle it over ¼ cup plus 1 tbsp (75 mL) cold water and stir to moisten it; let soften for 5 minutes.) Squeeze the water from the gelatin sheets and add them to the warm water; stir to dissolve. Stir the gelatin mixture into the warm purée mixture (or stir in the softened powdered gelatin, if using, until fully melted). Pour the entire mixture into the heart-shaped silicone mold and place it in the freezer for at least 3 hours.

* Make the Plougastel sponge cake (1). Preheat the oven to 350°F/180°C. Line a baking sheet with parchment paper and place the heart-shaped ring on top.

* In a large bowl, combine the almond flour, 1 (1 oz/30 g) egg white, and the confectioners' sugar using a silicone spatula (2).

* In the bowl of a standing mixer fitted with the whisk attachment, beat the remaining egg whites into stiff peaks, adding the sugar a little at a time halfway through the beating time (3).

* Using a silicone spatula, fold the meringue into the almond flour mixture (4).

* Fold in the sifted flour (5), then scrape the batter into a pastry bag fitted with a plain pastry tube.

* Pipe the batter into the heart-shaped ring (6).

* Bake for 10 minutes. Unmold the cake once cooled.

Saint-Valentin

VALENTINE'S DAY RASPBERRY-FILLED MOUSSE CAKE

* Make the white chocolate mousse. In a medium bowl, whisk together the egg yolks, cornstarch, and sugar (7). In a small saucepan, warm the milk, then pour it into the mixture while whisking constantly (8).

* Pour the entire mixture back into the saucepan and cook over very low heat, stirring constantly, until the mixture coats the back of the spoon, about 5 minutes (9).

* Soak the gelatin sheet for 10 minutes in a bowl of cold water. (If using powdered gelatin, sprinkle it over 1 tbsp plus 2 tsp (25 mL) cold water and stir to moisten it; let soften for 5 minutes.) Squeeze the water from the gelatin sheet and add it to the warm water; stir to dissolve. Stir the gelatin mixture into the warm custard (or stir in the softened powdered gelatin, if using, until fully melted).

* Place the chocolate in a large bowl and pour the warm gelatin mixture over the top (10) then stir until smooth and let cool slightly (11).

* Whip the cream into soft peaks and fold it delicately into the cooled mixture using a silicone spatula (12).

* Quickly begin assembling the cake before the mousse starts to set (13).

* Assemble the Saint-Valentin. Place the sponge cake in the cake ring, which has been placed on a serving plate. Pipe a line of mousse around the edge using a pastry bag fitted with a large plain pastry tube (14).

* Place the frozen raspberry center on top, centered (15).

* Pour the remaining mousse into the mold (16) and spread it out evenly (17).

* Freeze for 2 to 3 hours.

* The next day, make the glaze. In a small saucepan, heat the cream. Soak the gelatin sheet for 10 minutes in a bowl of cold water. (If using powdered gelatin, sprinkle it over 2 tsp (10 mL) cold water and stir to moisten it; let soften for 5 minutes). Squeeze the water from the gelatin sheet and add it to the warm water; stir to dissolve. Stir the gelatin mixture into the warm cream (or stir in the softened powdered gelatin, if using, until fully melted).

* Place the chocolate in a large bowl and pour the warm mixture over the top (18).

* Let sit for several minutes. Blend until smooth using an immersion blender. Let cool slightly (19).

* Unmold the cake onto a wire rack set over a sheet pan (20) and pour the glaze over the top (21).

* Immediately add several drops of the food color onto the freshly poured glaze (22), then carefully spread it out using a spatula to create a marbled effect (23). (You can also tint the entire glaze pink before pouring it onto the cake, as in the photo on page 209.)

* Place several raspberries on top and refrigerate the cake while it is still on the wire rack (24).

* Transfer the cake to a serving plate once the glaze has stopped dripping. Refrigerate until ready to serve.

Saint-Valentin

VALENTINE'S DAY RASPBERRY-FILLED MOUSSE CAKE

Galette des Rois

MARDI GRAS KING CAKE

SERVES
6 to 8

PREPARATION TIME: 20 minutes (not including the puff pastry dough) • COOKING TIME: 40 minutes

FOR THE ALMOND CREAM FILLING: 1 stick minus 1 tbsp (3 ½ oz/100 g) unsalted butter, room temperature • ½ cup (3 ½ oz/100 g) granulated sugar • 2 large (3 ½ oz/100 g) eggs • ¾ cup minus 1 ½ tsp (3 ½ oz/100 g) almond flour • 1 tbsp (⅓ oz/10 g) cornstarch • 1 tbsp (15 mL) rum

FOR THE GALETTE: 1 ¾ lb (800 g) all-butter puff pastry dough, homemade (see page 134) or store-bought, fresh or frozen • 1 dried lima bean • 1 large (⅔ oz/19 g) egg yolk

* Make the almond cream. In the bowl of a standing mixer fitted with the paddle attachment, beat the butter with the sugar until creamy. Add the eggs, almond flour, cornstarch, and rum, beating just until combined after each addition.

* Make the galette. Preheat the oven to 375°F/ 190°C. Line a baking sheet with parchment paper. Roll out the puff pastry dough to a thickness of ⅛ in (3 mm) and cut out two 9 ½-in (24-cm) circles. Place one of the circles on the baking sheet.

* Spread the almond cream on top, leaving a ¾-in (2-cm) border, then place the bean in a randomly selected spot on top of the cream.

* Combine the egg yolk with 1 tsp (5 mL) water and brush it around the edges of the dough with a pastry brush. Place the second dough circle on top, even with the edges of the bottom circle.

* Gently press the edges together to seal the layers, then generously brush the top with the egg wash.

* Using a very sharp blade, score the top of the cake in a decorative pattern of your choice, being careful not to cut all the way through the dough.

* Bake for 40 minutes, or until golden and flaky.

Galette des Rois au Chocolat et aux Noix de Pecan

CHOCOLATE-PECAN MARDI GRAS KING CAKE

★ ★ ★

SERVES
6 to 8

PREPARATION TIME: 20 minutes (not including the puff pastry dough) · COOKING TIME: 40 minutes

FOR THE MILK CHOCOLATE ALMOND CREAM: 5 ¼ oz (150 g) milk chocolate, in disks or evenly chopped · ½ stick plus 1 tbsp plus 2 tsp (3 oz/80 g) unsalted butter, room temperature · ¼ cup plus 2 tbsp plus 1 ¼ tsp (3 oz/80 g) granulated sugar · 2 large (3 ½ oz/100 g) eggs · ½ cup plus 1 tbsp (3 oz/80 g) almond flour · 1 tbsp (⅓ oz/10 g) cornstarch · 1 cup (4 ½ oz/125 g) pecans, coarsely chopped
FOR THE GALETTE: 1 ¾ lb (800 g) all-butter puff pastry dough homemade (see page 134) or store-bought, fresh or frozen · 1 dried lima bean · 1 large (⅔ oz/19 g) egg yolk

* Make the milk chocolate almond cream. In a large heatproof bowl set over a pot of simmering water, gently melt the chocolate (or place it in a microwave-safe bowl and microwave for 1 minute), then stir until completely melted. In the bowl of a standing mixer fitted with the paddle attachment, beat the butter with the sugar until creamy. Add the eggs, almond flour, cornstarch, and melted chocolate, beating just until combined after each addition.

* Make the galette. Preheat the oven to 375°F/190°C. Line a baking sheet with parchment paper. Roll out the puff pastry dough to a thickness of ⅛ in (3 mm) and cut out two 9 ½-in (24-cm) squares. Place one of the squares on the baking sheet.

* Spread the chocolate almond cream on top leaving a ¾-in (2-cm) border, then sprinkle the pecans on top. Place the bean in a randomly selected spot on top of the cream.

* Combine the egg yolk with 1 tsp (5 mL) water and brush it around the edges of the dough with a pastry brush. Place the second dough square on top, even with the edges of the bottom square. Gently press the edges of the dough together to seal the layers then generously brush the top with the egg wash.

* Using a very sharp blade, score the top of the cake in a decorative pattern of your choice, being careful not to cut all the way through the dough.

* Bake for 40 minutes, or until golden and flaky.

Nid de Pâques

CHOCOLATE NEST EASTER CAKE

★ ★ ★

SERVES
6 to 8

PREPARATION TIME: 1 hour · FREEZING TIME: Overnight, plus 1 hour
COOKING TIME: 17 minutes · REFRIGERATION TIME: 3 hours
One 8-in (20-cm) metal cake ring and one 7-in (18-cm) round silicone mold

FOR THE CHOCOLATE CRÉMEUX CENTER: 2 oz (55 g) premium couverture dark chocolate, in disks or evenly chopped · 1 large (2/3 oz/19 g) egg yolk · 1 tbsp (1/2 oz/13 g) granulated sugar · 3 tbsp plus 1 tsp (50 mL) whole milk · 3 tbsp plus 1 tsp (50 mL) heavy whipping cream

FOR THE CHOCOLATE NEST: 10 1/2 oz (300 g) premium couverture white chocolate, in disks or evenly chopped · Unsweetened cocoa powder, for dusting

FOR THE COCOA SPONGE CAKE: 2 large (3 1/2 oz/100 g) eggs, separated · 1/2 cup plus 1 tbsp plus 1/2 tsp (4 oz/115 g) granulated sugar, divided · 1/4 cup minus 1/2 tsp (3/4 oz/20 g) unsweetened cocoa powder, sifted

FOR THE GLAZE: 1 (1/10 oz/3 g) gelatin sheet, or 1 tsp (1/10 oz/3 g) powdered gelatin · 1 3/4 oz (50 g) premium couverture dark chocolate, in disks or evenly chopped · 1 oz (25 g) premium couverture milk chocolate, in disks or evenly chopped · 3 tbsp plus 1 tsp (50 mL) heavy whipping cream · 2 tbsp (30 mL) very warm water · 3 1/2 oz (100 g) neutral glaze

FOR THE CHOCOLATE MOUSSE: 4 (1/2 oz/12 g) gelatin sheets, or 1 tbsp plus 1 tsp (1/2 oz/12 g) powdered gelatin · 1 cup minus 2 1/2 tsp (6 2/3 oz/190 g) granulated sugar · 10 large (6 2/3 oz/190 g) egg yolks · 1 tbsp (15 mL) very warm water · 2 oz (55 g) premium couverture dark chocolate, in disks or evenly chopped · 1 3/4 oz (50 g) premium couverture milk chocolate, in disks or evenly chopped · 1/4 cup plus 2 1/2 tbsp (100 mL) heavy whipping cream, well chilled

FOR THE DECORATION: cocoa powder · chocoate Easter egg candies in different sizes

◦ The day before serving, make the chocolate crémeux center. Place the chocolate in a large bowl. In a medium bowl, vigorously whisk together the egg yolk and sugar. In a saucepan, warm the milk with the cream, then slowly pour the milk mixture into the egg mixture while whisking constantly. Pour the entire mixture back into the saucepan and cook over very low heat, stirring constantly, until the mixture coats the back of the spoon, about 5 minutes. Pour this mixture on top of the chocolate and stir until smooth. Let cool slightly.

◦ Blend using an immersion blender until completely smooth. Pour the mixture into the 7-in (18-cm) silicone mold and freeze until the next day.

◦ Make the chocolate nest. Place the chocolate in a large bowl.

Draw a 7-in (18-cm) circle on a piece of parchment paper; invert the paper (the lines should be visible) and place it on top of a serving plate.

◦ Bring a small saucepan of water to a simmer, then turn off the heat. Place the bowl on top of the saucepan (the water should not touch the bottom of the bowl) and cover it. Let the chocolate partially melt without stirring it.

◦ When the chocolate is almost melted, stir it gently and scrape it into a pastry bag fitted with a very fine round pastry tip. Using the parchment circle as a guide, pipe the chocolate into imperfect, stacked circles to form the shape of a bird's nest or crown (see photo). Refrigerate overnight, or until fully set and ready to assemble the cake.

Nid de Pâques

CHOCOLATE NEST EASTER CAKE

* Make the cocoa sponge cake. Preheat the oven to 425°F/220°C. Line a rimmed baking sheet with parchment paper.

* In the bowl of a standing mixer fitted with the whisk attachment, beat the egg whites until soft peaks form, then add half the sugar a little at a time halfway through the beating time and beat into stiff peaks.

* In a large bowl, whisk together the egg yolks and the remaining sugar until lightened, then whisk in the cocoa. Carefully fold the meringue into this mixture using a silicone spatula.

* Spread the batter in a thin layer on the prepared baking sheet and bake for 12 minutes. Cool completely. Carefully peel the parchment paper from the cake. Wrap tightly in plastic wrap and refrigerate until ready to assemble the cake.

* Make the glaze. Soak the gelatin sheet for 10 minutes in a bowl of cold water. (If using powdered gelatin, sprinkle it over 1 tbsp plus 2 tsp (25 mL) cold water and stir to moisten it; let soften for 5 minutes.)

* Place the dark and milk chocolate together in a large bowl. In a small saucepan, bring the cream to a boil. Squeeze the water from the gelatin sheet and add it to the warm water; stir to dissolve. Stir the gelatin mixture into the hot cream (or stir in the softened powdered gelatin, if using, until fully melted). Pour the gelatin mixture over the chocolate. Blend using an immersion blender, then stir in the neutral glaze until smooth. Cover the surface with plastic wrap and refrigerate overnight.

* The next day, assemble the cake. Make the chocolate mousse. Soak the gelatin sheets for 10 minutes in a bowl of cold water. (If using powdered gelatin, sprinkle it over ¼ cup plus 2½ tbsp (100 mL) cold water and stir to moisten it; let soften for 5 minutes.)

* In a small heavy saucepan, heat the sugar and 3 tbsp plus 1 tsp (50 mL) water over high heat to 250°F/121°C (if you do not have a candy thermometer, drop a small quantity of the hot syrup into a bowl of cold water. It should form a ball and feel soft when pinched between your fingers).

* In the bowl of a standing mixer fitted with the whisk attachment, begin beating the egg yolks. When the syrup reaches 250°F/121°C, pour it in a steady stream down the inside edge of the bowl with the mixer on medium speed and continue beating until the mixture is creamy.

* Squeeze the water from the gelatin sheets and add them to the warm water; stir to dissolve. Stir the gelatin mixture into the egg yolk mixture (or stir in the softened powdered gelatin, if using, until fully melted).

* In a large heatproof bowl set over a pot of simmering water, gently melt the dark and milk chocolate (or place it in a microwave-safe bowl and microwave for 1 minute), then stir to melt completely. Let cool slightly.

* Whip the cream to soft peaks. Using a silicone spatula, fold a small amount of it into the melted chocolate to lighten it; fold in the rest. Combine this mixture with the egg yolk-gelatin mixture.

* Cut out a disk of the sponge cake using the 8-in (20-cm) cake ring and place the ring on a serving plate. Place the cake in the bottom of the ring.

* Unmold the frozen crémeux center layer, then place it on top of the cake layer. Scrape the mousse into the ring and spread it out evenly to cover the layers. Freeze for 1 hour. Remove the ring.

* Place the cake on a wire rack set over a sheet pan. Warm the glaze in a heatproof bowl over a pot of simmering water, then pour it over the cake to cover it completely.

* Refrigerate for at least 3 hours to thaw. Just before serving, lightly dust the chocolate nest with cocoa, then place it on top of the cake. Place chocolate egg candies on top for decoration.

Les Gâteaux sans Gluten

GLUTEN-FREE COOKIES AND LOAVES

Cake à la Pistache sans Gluten

GLUTEN-FREE PISTACHIO LOAF CAKE

★ ★ ★

SERVES
6 to 8

PREPARATION TIME: 10 minutes · COOKING TIME: 30 minutes
One loaf pan measuring 8 in (22 cm) by 4 in (10 cm)

- 1 stick minus 1 tbsp (3 ½ oz/100 g) unsalted butter
- 4 large (7 oz/200 g) eggs, separated
- ½ cup plus 1 tbsp plus 1 ¾ tsp (4 ¼ oz/120 g) granulated sugar
- 3 tbsp (1 oz/25 g) almond flour
- 1 ¾ oz (50 g) pistachio paste
- ¾ cup (4 ¼ oz/120 g) rice flour
- ½ tsp (1/10 oz/2 g) baking powder
- 3 tbsp (1 oz/30 g) pistachios, chopped

* Preheat the oven to 325°F/165°C. Grease and flour the loaf pan.

* Melt the butter in a small saucepan or in a microwave-safe bowl. Place the egg yolks and sugar in a large mixing bowl or in the bowl of a standing mixer fitted with the whisk attachment. Beat until well combined, then beat in the melted butter, almond flour, and pistachio paste until well blended. With the mixer on low speed, beat in the rice flour and baking powder, just until incorporated and the mixture is smooth.

* Beat the egg whites into stiff peaks, then fold them into the batter. Scrape the batter into the prepared pan and sprinkle with the chopped pistachios.

* Bake for about 30 minutes or until dark golden on top (210°F/100°C on an instant-read thermometer). Do not overbake.

Cookies au Chocolat et Graines de Sésame sans Gluten

GLUTEN-FREE CHOCOLATE-SESAME COOKIES

★ ★ ★

MAKES ABOUT
18
COOKIES

PREPARATION TIME: 15 minutess · COOKING TIME: 10 to 12 minutes

1¼ cups (6⅔ oz/190 g) rice flour · 3 tbsp (1 oz/25 g) almond flour · 1¼ tsp (⅛ oz/5 g) baking powder · ⅔ cup (3⅛ oz/90 g) potato starch · 1 tsp (¼ oz/6 g) salt · 2 sticks minus 1 tsp (7¾ oz/220 g) unsalted butter, room temperature · 1¼ cups (9⅔ oz/275 g) light brown sugar · 2 large (3½ oz/100 g) eggs · 9 oz (260 g) premium couverture dark chocolate, in disks or evenly chopped · ½ cup (3⅛ oz/90 g) sesame seeds

* Preheat the oven to 325°F/160°C. Line a baking sheet with parchment paper.

* In a large bowl, whisk together the rice four, almond flour, baking powder, potato starch, and salt.

* In the bowl of a standing mixer fitted with the paddle attachment, beat the butter with the brown sugar until creamy. Beat in the eggs just until incorporated. Reduce the speed to low and beat in the flour mixture just until incorporated.

* In a large heatproof bowl set over a pot of simmering water, gently melt the chocolate (or place it in a microwave-safe bowl and microwave it for 1 minute), then stir to melt it completely. Carefully incorporate it into the batter.

* Scoop out the dough in heaping tablespoonfuls and quickly roll between your palms into balls. Set the balls at least 2 in (5 cm) apart on the prepared baking sheet. Sprinkle the balls with sesame seeds.

* Bake for 10 to 12 minutes, depending on the size of the cookies; they should be dry around the edges but still moist in the center. Let cool slightly before removing them from the baking sheet.

Cookies au Muesli sans Gluten

GLUTEN-FREE MUESLI COOKIES

MAKES ABOUT 18 COOKIES

PREPARATION TIME: 10 minutes · COOKING TIME: 10 to 12 minutes

- 1⅓ cups plus 1 tbsp (7½ oz/210 g) rice flour
- 2 cups minus 3 tbsp (7½ oz/210 g) buckwheat flour
- 2 tbsp plus 1 tsp (¾ oz/20 g) almond flour
- ¾ cup (3⅔ oz/105 g) potato starch
- 1¼ tsp (⅛ oz/5 g) baking powder
- 2 pinches salt
- 2½ sticks plus 1 tbsp (10½ oz/300 g) unsalted butter, room temperature
- 3 tbsp plus 1 tsp (50 mL) olive oil
- 1⅔ cups (12⅔ oz/360 g) light brown sugar
- 2 large (3½ oz/100 g) eggs
- 1⅓ cups (7 oz/200 g) raisins
- 3½ oz (100 g) dried apricots, diced
- 3⅛ oz (90 g) mixed seeds, such as sesame, sunflower, and pumpkin

* Preheat the oven to 325°F/160°C. Line a baking sheet with parchment paper.

* In a large bowl, whisk together the rice flour, buckwheat flour, almond flour, potato starch, baking powder, and salt.

* In the bowl of a standing mixer fitted with the paddle attachment, beat together the butter, oil, and brown sugar until smooth and creamy. Beat in the eggs just until incorporated.

* Combine the flour mixture with the egg mixture just until incorporated. Fold in the raisins and dried apricots using a silicone spatula.

* Scoop out the dough in heaping tablespoonfuls and quickly roll between your palms into balls. Set the balls at least 2 in (5 cm) apart on the baking sheet. Sprinkle with the seeds.

* Bake for 10 to 12 minutes, depending on the size of the cookies; they should be dry around the edges but still moist in the center. Let cool slightly before removing them from the baking sheet.

Cake au Chocolat et aux Noisettes sans Gluten

GLUTEN-FREE CHOCOLATE-HAZELNUT LOAF CAKE

★ ★ ★

SERVES
6 to 8

PREPARATION TIME: 10 minutes · COOKING TIME: 25 minutes · One loaf pan measuring 8 in (22 cm) by 4 in (10 cm)

FOR THE BATTER: ¼ cup plus 1 tbsp plus 1¾ tsp (2½ oz/70 g) granulated sugar · 4 large (7 oz/200 g) eggs · 7 oz (200 g) dark chocolate, in disks or evenly chopped · ½ stick plus 1 tbsp (2½ oz/70 g) unsalted butter · ½ cup minus 1 tbsp (2½ oz/70 g) rice flour · 1¾ oz (50 g) chocolate chips

FOR THE GLAZE: 3⅛ oz (90 g) premium couverture dark chocolate, in disks or evenly chopped · 2 tbsp (1 oz/30 g) unsalted butter · ⅓ cup (1¾ oz/50 g) whole hazelnuts or almonds, crushed

· Preheat the oven to 325°F/165°C. Grease and flour the loaf pan.

· Place the sugar and the eggs in a large bowl or in the bowl of a standing mixer fitted with the whisk attachment. Beat for several minutes on low speed until foamy.

· In a large heatproof bowl set over a pot of simmering water, gently melt the chocolate and the butter together (or place them in a microwave-safe bowl and microwave for 1 minute), then stir to melt completely. Let cool slightly. With the mixer on low speed, beat the chocolate mixture into the egg mixture. Add the rice flour and beat again just until incorporated

and the batter is smooth. Using a spatula, fold in the chocolate chips.

· Scrape the batter into the prepared pan and bake for about 25 minutes, or until golden on top (210°F/100°C on an instant-read thermometer). Do not overbake.

· Let cool. Unmold the loaf and place it on a wire rack set over a sheet pan.

· Make the glaze. In a heatproof bowl set over a pot of simmering water, gently melt the chocolate with the butter (or place them in a microwave-safe bowl and microwave for 1 minute), stir until smooth, and pour it over the cake.

· Sprinkle with the chopped hazelnuts or almonds.

Moelleux au Chocolat sans Gluten

GLUTEN-FREE MOLTEN CHOCOLATE CAKE

★ ★ ★

SERVES
6 to 8

PREPARATION TIME: 10 minutes · COOKING TIME: 13 to 18 minutes, depending on the size of the cake
One 7-in (18-cm) round cake pan or six 3-in (8-cm) round baking pans

- 7 oz (200 g) 70% cacao dark chocolate, in disks or evenly chopped
- ½ stick plus 1 tbsp (2 ½ oz/70 g) unsalted butter
- 4 large (7 oz/200 g) eggs
- ¼ cup plus 1 tbsp plus 1¾ tsp (2 ½ oz/70 g) granulated sugar
- ½ cup minus 1 tbsp (2 ½ oz/70 g) rice flour

* Preheat the oven to 300°F/150°C. Grease and flour the pan (if using a silicone pan, there is no need to grease or flour it).

* In a large heatproof bowl set over a pot of simmering water, gently melt the chocolate and the butter together (or place them in a microwave-safe bowl and microwave for 1 minute), then stir to melt completely.

* In a large bowl, whisk the eggs and sugar together until lightened. Add the chocolate mixture and stir to combine.

* Whisk in the rice flour, just until incorporated and the mixture is smooth.

* Scrape the batter into the prepared pan and bake for 13 to 18 minutes (do not overbake; cake should be soft and moist).

* Let cool. Unmold onto a serving plate.

Recipe Index

Bûche au Café

Chouquettes

Diamants au Chocolat

Éclairs au Chocolat

Galette des Rois

Gâteau Basque

Kugelhopf

Macaronnade

Mi-cuit au Chocolat

Mille-Feuille

Pain d'Épices aux Fruits

Paris-Brest

Succès

Tarte au Caramel et au
Chocolat au Lait

Tarte Monge

Tout-Choco